Exploring Intel® Edison

Using C and the Mini-Breakout Board

Harry Fairhead

I/O Press
I Programmer Library

Exploring Intel® Edison

Copyright © 2016 IO Press

Harry Fairhead, *Exploring Intel® Edison Using C and the Mini-Breakout Board*

ISBN Paperback: 978-1-871962-44-4

First Edition
First Printing, 2016
Revision 1

Published by IO Press   www.iopress.info
In association with I Programmer   www.i-programmer.info
and with I o T Programmer   www.iot-programmer.com

Preface

This is an introduction to using the Intel Edison in C using the Mini-breakout board. It is expected that you know how to program, but not necessarily in C, and that you also have an idea how electronics works but you don't have to be an expert.

I haven't given exact instructions about how circuits should be built as we all have our own preferred ways of working. My aim, however, was to make best use of the Edison's unique properties – mainly its size. Rather than use the Arduino breakout board with all of its additional interfaces, I have used the Edison "raw". This is a little more difficult than pretending that it is an Arduino, but it is the only way to design things that cannot be so easily built using an Arduino-like device.

I have also avoided using higher level languages than C – notably Python – for the simple reason that this is one area where you often need the maximum speed that can be coaxed out of a processor. You can use C++ and Python if you want to, and for some tasks this is appropriate, but for the sort of things that this book concentrates on C is the most appropriate language.

The other key decision is how to actually access the hardware. Instead of using a high level upm library, which is an object-oriented, device-based library we use something simpler – mraa. This is a cross-platform approach to giving access to GPIO lines and other I/O protocols such as SPI. It can be used from C or via a C++ wrapper. The reason for using mraa in C is simply another aspect of the search for maximum speed and efficiency. After you have things working in C using mraa you can chose to either drop down a level and get rid of all library code or move up to C++ and encapsulate what you are doing as a upm module.

If you have a device that is in the upm library then the temptation is to simply use it and this is reasonable, but if you really want to know how it all works then implement the protocol yourself, this is the approach taken in much of this book.

My grateful thanks are due to the Intel Edison team who kindly provided support and input to the development of this book.

For updates, errata, links to resources and the source code for the programs in this book visit its dedicated page on the IoT Programmer website:

http://www.iot-programmer.com/index.php/books/exploring-edison

Table of Contents

Chapter 1   **9**
Why the Intel Edison?
      Meet Edison..9
      The Edison Architecture..10
      Standard Breakout Boards...12
      Arduino Breakout Board..12
      Edison (Mini) Breakout Board......................................14
      Which Breakout?..16

Chapter 2   **17**
Getting Started
      The Hardware...17
      Integrated Installers...19
      The Serial Port..19
      Updating the System...21
      Setting Up WiFi..22
      Updating the Mraa Library...23
      Pulse a Pin..24
      Programming the Edison..25
      Summary..26

Chapter 3   **27**
In C
      Installing Eclipse...28
      A First Project...29
      Remote Systems...31
      The Program..32
      Debugging...36
      Summary..38

Chapter 4   **39**
Mraa GPIO
      Pin Numbering...39
      Drive Characteristics..42
      Output...43
      Phased Pulses...44
      Basic Input..46
      Interrupts..47
      How Edison Interrupts Work..49
      Pulse Width Measurement..50
      Summary..53

Chapter 5   **55**
Fast Memory Mapped I/O
    How Fast?..56
    Delay Using usleep...57
    Busy wait...58
    Fast Mapped I/O..59
    Fast Input...63
    Direct Memory Mapping..67
    Summary..69

Chapter 6   **71**
Near Realtime Linux
    The Problem..71
    Realtime Scheduling...73
    Setting Scheduling Priority...74
    How Bad Is The Problem?...75
    Realtime FIFO Scheduling..77
    Practical FIFO Scheduling..79
    Summary..80

Chapter 7   **81**
Pulse Width Modulation – PWM
    Some Basic Edison PWM Facts....................................81
    Mraa PWM commands...82
    Using PWM...85
    How Fast?..86
    Uses of PWM – Driving LEDs....................................87
    Changing the LED Brightness.....................................90
    Controlling a Servo...91
    What Else Can You Use PWM For?............................94
    Summary..94

Chapter 8   **95**
Getting Started with the I2C Bus
    I2C Hardware Basics 95
    Edison I2C 97
    The I2C Mraa Functions...98
    Slow Read...101
    SYSFS Linux I2C Commands...................................102
    Summary..103

Chapter 9   **105**
I2C Measuring Temperature
    The SparkFun HTU21D..105
    Wiring the HTU21D..106
    A First Program 106
    In Detail...108
    Reading the Raw Temperature Data..109
    Processing the Data..111
    Reading the Humidity..112
    Checksum Calculation..112
    Complete Listing..113
    Summary..114

Chapter 10   **115**
Life At 1.8V
    Logic Levels...115
    Output 1.8V To 3.3V and 5V..116
    Output Level Conversion...117
    5V and 3.3V to 1.8V input...120
    Bi-directional Bus..121
    Summary..125

Chapter 11   **127**
Using the DHT11/22 Temperature Humidity Sensor at 1.8V
    The Device...127
    The Electronics..129
    The Software..131
    Reading the Data...132
    Complete Listing..135
    Summary..136

Chapter 12   **137**
The DS18B20 1-Wire Temperature
    The Hardware..137
    Initialization 141
    Writing Bits...143
    A First Command..145
    Reading Bits..146
    Initiating A Temperature Conversion...147
    Reading the Scratchpad...148
    Getting the Temperature...149
    Complete Listing..150
    Summary..152

Chapter 13   **153**
Using The SPI Bus
    SPI Bus Basics..153
    The SPI Functions..157
    A Loop Back Example...160
    Some Edison SPI Problems..162
    A User Mode Driver...164
    Implementing the User Mode Driver............................165
    General SPI Problems..169
    Summary 169

Chapter 14   **171**
SPI In Practice with the MCP3008 AtoD
    The MCP3008..171
    Connecting MCP3008 to Edison....................................173
    Basic Configuration..175
    The Protocol...176
    Some Packaged Functions..177
    How Fast..178
    Using Software SPI Emulation......................................179
    Listing Of Soft SPI Program..182
    Summary..185

Chapter 15   **187**
Beyond Mraa- Controlling Features It Doesn't
    Working with SYSFS..187
    Example – toggling a line..189
    Controlling the GPIO Mode..190
    The Output Modes...192
    Setting the Mode...193
    Summary..196

Chapter 1

Why the Intel Edison?

The Intel Edison is a very attractive single board computer for IoT projects. It has WiFi and Bluetooth as standard and it's cheap. The only minor downside is the it doesn't seem quite as easy to use as an Arduino, but when you understand it a little better you'll find it is both flexible and powerful.

It can be used as a powerful server or as a simple microcontroller, or both at the same time.

Meet Edison

The Intel Edison is remarkable because it is small, uses little power and yet has a lot of computing in a tiny SD card-sized board. It is a core component in Intel's Internet of Things (IoT) initiative where it has a large role to play.

At around $50 an Edison it isn't as cheap as an Arduino or a Raspberry Pi, but it has enough advantages over both to make it a sensible choice for many applications. Also, when you include the cost of the extras needed to provide WiFi and Bluetooth for the other two, then it is price is more comparable.

More to the point there are situations where its small size and low power consumption make it the only sensible choice.

However, the Edison is a little different from the alternatives and you need to know a little more about its characteristics and the best ways to make use of it depending on what you are trying to achieve.

The Edison is a full computer, but without a video or keyboard interface. This means you have to work with it via a remote console – connected via a serial/usb or network connection. Connections to the outside world can be via the built in WiFi, Bluetooth, serial port or USB. Even though it runs Linux it doesn't have a desktop environment only a command line. Even though it doesn't have video hardware it is a complete Linux machine and can be used as a server but this aspect is not the focus of this book.

It has 40 digital GPIO connections, but no analog I/O. No analog I/O might sound like a problem, but for such a small form factor this isn't surprising.

All of the connections to the Edison are made via a tiny 70-pin I/O connector. If you are used to wiring jumper wires directly to a Raspberry Pi or to an Arduino you will need to think again. The connector is intended not for direct connection but to connect to another PCB. For prototyping you need to use a breakout board and for a finished product you would create a custom board.

If you plan to use a prototype as a one-off finished device then you need to keep in mind that the need for a breakout board increases the size and cost.

The Edison Architecture

You can see the general structure of the Intel Edison in the diagram below:

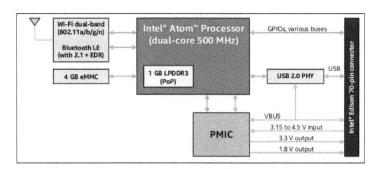

You can see that the dual core 500MHz Atom processor has access to memory, WiFi, Bluetooth LE, USB and to the GPIO (general purpose input/output) pins. You can write programs that work with all of these facilities. The Atom generally runs Yocto Linux, which you can treat as a fairly standard Linux for most of the time.

One little appreciated feature of the Edison is that it has two separate processors – the Atom Host CPU and a Quark processor acting as an MCU, Microprocessor Control Unit.

The MCU is a separate small CPU that handles the interfacing with the outside world. Most of the time you can ignore it because the main Atom processor talks to it on your behalf. The dual core Atom runs the Linux OS and the MCU is the microcontroller in the system running its own RTOS derived operating system. The MCU is a full 32 bit Intel Quark

10

microcontroller running at 100MHz, which makes it more powerful than your average microcontroller but you should not ignore the power of two full cores running at 500Mhz on the Atom processor.

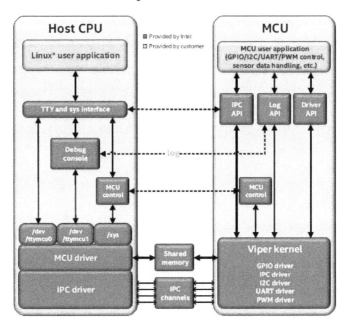

Until recently the SDK didn't provide access to the MCU. Instead the host CPU was the only thing you could program and so all Edison programs accessed the GPIO via programs written on the Atom processor running Linux. Now you can also write programs for the MCU that work with the GPIO lines without the need to involve the host CPU. What this means is that you can now use the MCU to preprocess the data and allow the Host to get on with higher level tasks.

For example, a slightly contrived example would be that the MCU could be programmed to pulse a line in Morse code corresponding to each letter of the alphabet. The Host processor could then simply pass the character to the MCU and expect it to get on with the task of sending the Morse code.

The division of labor here is typical of the way the Host and MCU can be used together. Of course not all, indeed not many applications need this sort of division of labor and in the main you can mostly concentrate on programming the host – which is what we are going to do in this book.

Standard Breakout Boards

The Edison has 40 GPIO connections – some of which have special roles like acting as a serial interface or interfacing to an SD card.

In a finished product you would wire directly to the 70-pin connector via your custom breakout board, but for prototyping you need something to give you access while you experiment.

The 70-pin connector brings out the GPIO lines, a USB port and the power lines. As already mentioned, the connector is very small 70-pin Hirose DF40 and with 0.4 mm contact pitch it is very difficult to solder to directly.

The solution is to use a breakout board which accepts the Edison and provides power and other facilities.

It is worth mentioning at this early stage that the Edison uses 1.8V logic, which means you can't simply attach an LED say and expect to toggle it on and off. The problem of converting the 1.8V logic levels to something more familiar is something that a breakout board can tackle.

There are two standard breakout boards from Intel and a number of similar ones from other sources. For simplicity let's look at just the Intel boards.

Arduino Breakout Board

The first is the Arduino breakout board. As its name suggests, this takes the GPIO connections from the Edison and converts them both electrically and physically to the outputs you would find on the Arduino. So exact is this mapping that you can actually use Arduino shields to expand the Edison.

When installed on an Arduino breakout board the Edison looks a lot like the Intel Galileo but with WiFi. This similarity between the Edison+Arduino board and Galileo explains why you will often find software and documentation covering both. While there are some differences, such as the WiFi, in most cases what works for the Galileo should work with the Edison plus Arduino breakout board.

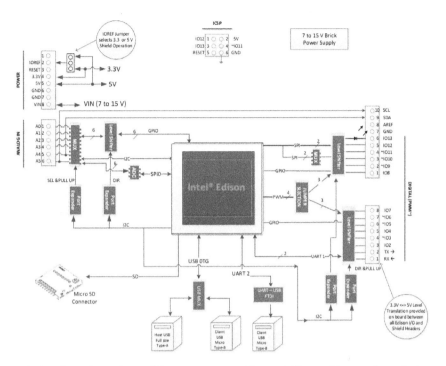

The Arduino breakout board is easy to use. Especially so if you already have Arduino experience. The reason is that one of the possible programming environments for the Edison is the Arduino IDE which allows you to write programs as if you were working with a real Arduino. That is, the Arduino breakout board allows you to treat the Edison as if it was an Arduino for much of the time - for both hardware and software.

The Arduino breakout board also provides lots of extras that make getting started with the Edison easier. In particular it provides logic level translation from 1.8V to the more familiar 5V. This allows you to directly connect and flash LEDs and use the sensors output devices that you might well be familiar with.

Of course if you are thinking of creating a custom device based on the Edison then the Arduino board may present you with a small problem. It implements electronics to convert the Edison GPIO to the Arduino pin out. If you want to move on from using the breakout board then you are going to have to duplicate any of the electronics on the breakout board that supports Arduino features that you want to use that aren't native. For example, if you make use any of the AtoD converter pins then you have to implement one on your custom board. This isn't as difficult as it sounds because Intel have provided that full schematic of the Arduino breakout board and you can use this as the basis for your own.

Edison (Mini) Breakout Board

Using the Intel Edison as an Arduino has lots of advantages but there are times when the project you have in mind really doesn't need the fairly elaborate hardware that is used to implement the Arduino pinouts. In these cases it is better to make use of the much smaller Edison breakout board, referred to here the "mini-breakout" board. You can see from a block diagram this is a very much simpler breakout board than the Arduino board:

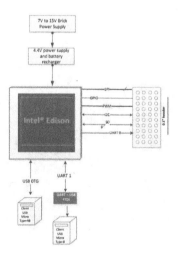

While the USB and power have some electronics dedicated to making them easier to use, the GPIO lines are brought out directly to a 0.1 inch header. Notice that you don't actually get any pins to connect to just the solder pads.

How to deal with this is depends on how you want to work but it is easy to solder some pins directly onto the board.

Also notice that there is no SD card – if you want to support an SD card you have to add some electronics to the SD lines available on the header. There are also no analog I/O lines and this can be a bigger problem but it is much easier than you might imagine to add low cost converters. The board is also much smaller than the Arduino breakout and more in keeping with the whole Edison ethos:

The mini-breakout board has all you need to power and talk to the Edison but it makes no effort to convert the Edison GPIO to anything at all. What you do get is the large header space on the bottom of the board. This is very easy to work with and you can make connection to a prototype board via jumper wires. What you do with the signals next is up to you, but it is worth mentioning again that the native logic level for the Edison is 1.8V and its current drive is just 3mA. In other words, these are not TTL or CMOS levels of the sort you encounter in the Arduino and the Raspberry Pi. For example, you can't just connect an LED to a pin and expect to be able to switch it on and off - the voltage is too low and there isn't enough drive current. It might work if you use an LED with a low drive demand but you cannot rely on it.

If you want to use a 5V sensor then this low voltage logic makes things more difficult, but many modern sensors use, or can use, a 1.8V logic level. The advantage of working with such low voltages is that the sensors and other devices use a lot less power. If you do want to use your favorite 5V sensor or output device then you are going to have to get used to implementing level shifting and drivers and this is something we have to tackle. It turns out to be not a huge problem as explained in Chapter 10 and once you have settled down with 1.8V logic it is as easy to live with as TTL or CMOS levels.

You can also use the Arduino IDE to develop software for the mini-breakout board. However in most cases it makes more sense to program your applications using C or Python, or even JavaScript and leave the Arduino behind. You can also use these languages with the Arduino IDE and move your programs over to the mini-breakout board very easily. In this way you can develop your code and be sure it works before you have to implement the custom hardware needed to make the mini-breakout board work properly. For example, if you want to create a new serial protocol using a GPIO line then you can use the Arduino board as a level shifter to 5V and develop your software. Then, knowing it works, you can move to the mini-breakout board and implement a 5V level shifter. If you use any of the features of the Arduino board, such as the AtoD converters, then again once you are sure your software works, all you have to do is implement AtoD in hardware for use with the mini-breakout.

In short the Arduino breakout board makes a good testbed for your mini-breakout projects, which in turn makes a good testbed for your final production device.

Which Breakout?

If you don't want to be troubled by hardware complications start with an Arduino breakout board. This not only gives you Arduino pinouts, but also level shifts the 1.8V logic of the Edison to the 5V logic of the Arduino. In addition you can use the full Arduino IDE to develop software. This means you can use all of the interfacing techniques you have learned in using the Arduino and Arduino projects are easy to move to the Edison. Judging by comments on forums, this seems to be, the route that most users are taking and hence there is a wealth of information available. However, if you think the Arduino board is for you you need to ask if a simpler solution might not be an Arduino proper. In most cases the Arduino board is best regarded as a stepping stone to the mini board. Put simply treating the Edison as an Arduino isn't making best use of it and is for the beginner.

If you can handle the minor complications involved in level shifting and generally working with 1.8V logic and want to create something small and low power then the mini-breakout board is for you. While you are going to have to implement any additional I/O facilities you need, as the mini-breakout board only provides you with the raw GPIO lines, this is not the big problem that it might appear to be. In fact in no time at all you should find it easy to not only to use new 1.8V sensors when they are available, but also to interface to your favorite 5V and 3.3V devices including bidirectional devices.

We are going to work with the mini-breakout board and deal with any extra difficulties we encounter as a result.

Chapter 2

Getting Started

The native, mini-breakout, board is harder to work with in some respects, but it is the one you need to master to get the real Edison experience.

In this chapter of Exploring Edison we work through the ideas need to get started with the mini-breakout board.

The mini-breakout board is the one that brings out the true nature of the Edison but the Arduino board is useful for checking that software works and gaining access to extended I/O without having to implement any special hardware.

The Hardware

Setting up the Edison with either of the Intel breakout boards is fairly straightforward and there isn't much that you have to do.

Get the Edison and plug it into the breakout board. Fix it into place using the nuts provided if you don't plan to remove it often. The next step is to find two USB cables (Micro B to A) or one USB cable and a power supply. When you are getting started it is probably easier to use the two USB cables as this powers the Edison and gives you access to its internal storage and other facilities.

At this point the question arises of why two cables. The answer is that both breakout boards both have two USB connectors – this is one respect in which they are similar. One of the connectors – on the inside - is a true USB port. The other - on the edge - is a serial interface converted to be a USB port.

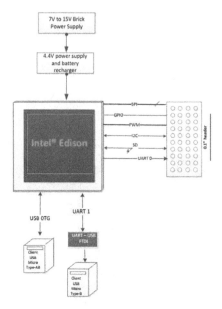

The true USB port can be used to power the system and it allow you to make a connection for doing things like downloading software and access the Edison's internal storage. The Serial USB port is used to connect a serial console so that you can "talk" to the Linux operating system. In practice you can avoid using one of the two USB connections but when you are starting it is best to just make use of them for simplicity of getting started.

On the mini-breakout board the sockets are easy to find:

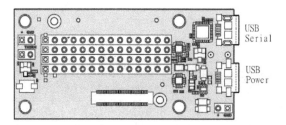

So all you have to do is plug two USB cables into the breakout board and into a suitable computer. If you do this you should see a green LED next to the Edison light up to indicate that power is on.

Depending on the OS you are using various drivers may have been automatically installed or you may have install them manually.

One thing that does get installed automatically on all systems is the Edison's internal drive. If everything is working you should be able to see an additional drive labeled "Edison" in whatever file manger you are using.

Let's deal in detail with the serial port first and start talking to the on-board Yocto Linux. At this stage you can more or less ignore the other USB socket and just treat it as a way of supplying power. You don't even have to install drivers for it until you want to make use of it.

Integrated Installers

If you are using Windows 64-bit, Linux or a Mac to develop Edison programs then there is a very easy way to get all of the drivers and software installed in one step – the Windows 64-bit, Linux or Mac OSX Integrated Installer, which can be downloaded from the Intel site:

   https://software.intel.com/en-us/iot/hardware/edison

The integrated installers make things so simple it really isn't worth doing the job manually. However it can help with debugging to know what they do.

If you run the installer it will install all the drivers needed in one operation and update the Edison's Linux image to the latest version. You can also optionally install any and all of the standard development IDEs.

The Integrated Installer takes some time to do its job so be patient. If it doesn't work, i.e. if it hangs or fails at some point, simply run it again. The installer can be used to up-date the software and/or repair it.

The Serial Port

The Edison's serial port is the way you connect a console with the Linux OS running on the device. As the serial port is converted by the breakout board to a USB connection, you need a USB serial driver installed on your PC.

If you are using **Linux** the USB serial port will be set up automatically as /dev/ttyUSB0.

If you are using **OSX** it will be set up automatically in /dev/tty. To find out which device it is using:

```
ls /dev/tty.*
```

and look for a device that has usbserial in its name, for example:

```
tty.usbserial-A402YSYU
```

Under **Windows** you will need to install a USB serial port driver. To do this either run the Integrated installer or download the FTDI driver, run the installer with admin privileges, use run as administrator. You should discover that a new USB Serial Port has been added. Use the device manager to discover its port number - usually USB Serial Port (COM3). If you have installed other drivers using the Integrated Installer you will also see a USB

Composite Device - ignore this for the moment, the port that you want is usually listed as USB Serial Port.

Next all you have to do is use a serial console to connect to the Edison. You can use any serial console to connect and the only thing you need to know is that the baud rate is 115200.

Under **Linux** and **OSX** you can use the screen command. Under **Linux** you might have to install it using:

```
sudo apt-get install screen
```

and then run it using:

```
sudo screen /dev/ttyUSB0 115200
```

Under **OSX** run the screen terminal using:

```
screen /dev/devname 115200 -L
```

where *devname* is the serial device you found earlier.

If you are using **Windows** then things are a little more difficult. You need a serial console but Windows 7 and later no longer come with one as standard. The simplest solution is to download PuTTY from:

http://www.chiark.greenend.org.uk/~sgtatham/putty/download.html

This is a very useful program as it not only works as a serial terminal but as a Telnet and SSH console. It is worth getting to know. Just download it and run the .exe file. There is no installation.

To use it to connect to the Edison simply run it and select serial connection. Enter the port that corresponds to the USB serial connection and set the speed to 115200:

You can save these details to make connecting easier in future. If it doesn't work, the only possible reasons are that you have the wrong com port or the wrong speed. The speed has to be 115200 and you can find the com port by trial and error if needs be.

No matter how you connect to the serial port, the next step is the same for all three operating systems. You might have to press carriage return twice to wake the session up, but you should then see the Yocto Linux sign-on banner. All you have to do is log in with the user name "root".

At this point you have made contact with the Edison and are working with the Linux operating system that it ships with.

In theory your next task is to up-date its firmware to make sure you are working with the latest version, but if you know some Linux commands you could have a look around the system first.

Updating the System

Updating the system is something you have to do before moving on. The latest version of the OS is essential if you are to be sure that things are going to work as documented. If you have installed the software using the Integrated Installer for Windows 64bit, Linux or OSX then the OS image will have been updated for you. You can also use the Integrated Installer to update the firmware by running it again and selecting that option.

If you run into difficulties or need to do something special such as reverting to an earlier OS image then you can download Flash Tool Lite. To use it you simply download the OS image that you want to use but don't bother to unzip it. Run the Flash Tool and use the browse button to specify the zipped image file you downloaded. Make sure the Edison is connected. The Flash Tool will unzip the system image and when you click Start Flash it will upload the image to the Edison. However it will ask you to unplug and plug the Edison back in so as to reboot it.

If you have any problems with the Edison being detected then try a USB 2.0 hub – there have been reports of problems with USB 3 ports.

Setting Up WiFi

Once you have the latest version of the operating system installed, your next task is to connect to WiFi.

If you have used the installer then you will have been given the opportunity to specify the network SSID and password. If you want to change the WiFi connection then the simplest way is to run the installer again. It is, however, useful to know how to change the WiFi connection manually.

Just use the command:

```
configure_edison -setup
```

and supply the information the utility requests. You have to provide a unique name for the device and you can optionally set a logon password.

It is important that you do supply a logon password because without one you can only securely connect (SSH) to the Edison via the serial port or the network over a USB connection. This means you cannot connect an SSH terminal or FTP client via WiFi. To allow SSH connections on all ports you have to either supply a password or manually alter the configuration.

As part of setting up the WiFi a scan is performed and you'll see this displayed on the screen:

```
Configure Edison:
WiFi ConnectionScanning: 1 seconds left
0 : Rescan for networks
1 : Manually input a hidden SSID
2 : MyNetwork
Enter 0 to rescan for networks.
Enter 1 to input a hidden network SSID.
Enter 2 to choose MyNetwork
```

All you have to do is enter the number corresponding to the network you want to connect to. You then have to provide the network's password and, if all goes well, you will see a message telling you the IP address and how to access the device:

```
Done. Please connect your laptop or PC to the same network as
this device and go to http://192.168.11.25 or
http://Edison1.local in your browser.
```

When you get to the web page all you will see is confirmation of the IP address and name:

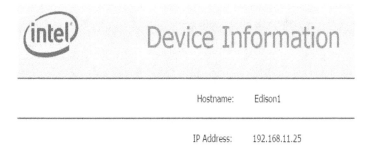

What really matters is that you have managed to get the Edison connected.

You can rerun the Configure_Edison utility any time you want to change the configuration. There are separate options for '—password" and "—wifi" if you just want to update a portion of your system configuration

Updating the Mraa Library

The mraa library is going to be very important, but it gets upgraded faster than the OS at the moment. You need to install the latest version before trying anything out. In particular, the mini-breakout board doesn't work unless you update to the current version.

If you have opted to use the latest version of the Eclipse IDE then simply starting a new project will check that the version of mraa on the Edison is the same as the one used locally — and this is usually the version you want to use. If this is the first time you have used the Eclipse IDE then it is a good idea to allow it to upgrade the libraries automatically.

Sometimes however you need to do the job manually. Fortunately it is a fairly easy procedure. For it to work you have to have connected the Edison to the Internet one way or another.

Then copy and paste the following at the Linux command prompt:

```
1. echo "src maa-
   upm http.//iotdk.intel.com/repos/1.1/intelgalactic" >
   /etc/opkg/intel-iotdk.conf
2. opkg update
3. opkg upgrade
```

For future reference opkg is the Yocto Linux package manager.

Following the upgrade, performed either by Eclipse or manually, all of the examples in the rest of this book should work.

If you download and install a new OS image then you have to check that the version of mraa you have is the very latest. The simplest way to discover the version of mraa you have installed is to use Python, or the language of your choice to call get_version.

To do this give the command:

```
python
```

Then in the Python REPL that appears type:

```
import mraa
```

and finally

```
mraa.getVersion()
```

Which will display something like:

```
'v0.5.4-110-g459ecc0'
```

You can compare this to the latest version listed on GitHub at: https://github.com/intel-iot-devkit/mraa/releases

Pulse a Pin

We are going to have to spend time getting a development environment set up, but it is still worth seeing how easy it is to control the Edison's GPIO pins. The key to it all is the mraa library, which allows you to access the GPIO, no matter which of the breakout boards you are using.

In fact mraa works on a range of other devices including the Galileo and the Raspberry Pi, so it is worth finding out about. It is a C/C++ library but it can also be used from Python or JavaScript.

To get us started, to check that everything is working, and just for a general confidence boost, we can work interactively in Python and flash an LED manually.

I say "flash an LED", but there is only a real LED to flash on the Arduino breakout board. On the mini-breakout board all we can do, without adding some components, is check the voltage level on one of the outputs.

First, we have to say something about how to determine which pin number corresponds to which physical pin. Mraa uses a standard set of pin numbers which are mapped to appropriate pins on different devices. There is a lot more to say about this, but all you need to know at the moment is that mraa pin number 13 is mapped to pin 13 on the Arduino breakout board, which has an LED connected, and to pin J17-14 on the mini-breakout board.

You don't need to find the pin on the Arduino breakout board because if everything works you will see the LED go on and off.

Finding the pin on the mini-breakout board is easy because the pin rows are labeled and pin J17-14 is the far left pin on the top row looking at the underside of the board:

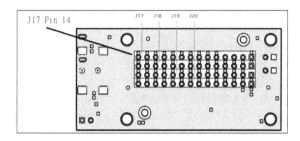

The simplest way to make sure that the pin state changes is to use a multimeter. If you don't have one get one at once, they are cheap and essential. You can make a ground connection using the through-plated mounting holes. Remember the logic levels are 0 and 1.8V and you will see zero when the pin is set to zero and 1.8 when it is set to 1. Also be careful not to short other pads or tracks on the PCB with the multimeter probes.

Programming the Edison

Now to the software. Open a serial connection and log in if you need to. To get the Python interpreter running simply type:

```
python
```

you should see a three-arrow >>> prompt appear. You can now type in any Python commands and they will be obeyed at once.

To load the mraa library use:

```
import mraa
```

if you see any error messages then the chances are that your mraa library isn't up-to-date -see above.

Next we need to create a pin object:

```
x = mraa.Gpio(13)
```

and set it to be an output

```
x.dir(mraa.DIR_OUT)
```

Now we can switch the pin to high:

```
x.write(1)
```

On the mini-breakout board you should measure 1.8V on pin J17-14.

To set the pin low use:

```
x.write(0)
```

The LED should go off and the voltage on pin J17-14 should drop to 0V.

That's all there is to it. You now have a working connected Edison and you can program its GPIO pins. Of course, there is a lot more to find out and master.

Summary

1. The Edison breakout boards have two USB connectors – one supplies power and other services and the other is a serial port allowing you to connect to the OS.

2. No matter which breakout board you are using connect both USB sockets to your host machine using suitable cables.

3. Even without additional drivers, all host machines should recognize the shared flash drive in the Edison as a hard disk with the device name Edison.

4. You can connect to the Edison using a serial console of your choice. Linux and OS X should have a suitable console and drivers for the USB port already installed.

5. If you are using Windows you need to download a USB Serial driver and a suitable serial console – Putty is probably the one to use.

6. Once you have made a serial connection you can log on to Yocto Linux using the user name "root" with no password.

7. It is important that you upgrade the OS to the latest version. Simply download the OS image and copy it to the shared drive. Then restart the Edison using reboot ota. The Edison will restart twice before the update is complete.

8. Use configure_edison --setup to connect to WiFi.

9. It is important to update the mraa library. Without the latest version things tend not to work.

10. With the upgraded mraa library you can now use C/C++, Python or JavaScript to control the Edison's GPIO.

Chapter 3

In C

You have a choice of languages that you can use with the Edison, but there are big advantages to choosing C or C++ for bigger projects. If you know Python or JavaScript then you will find it very easy to make the switch. So let's do it in C.

Before we get started, it needs to be made clear why it is worth learning how to use the Edison in C. You can use languages such as Python and JavaScript and I have a great fondness for both. The reason for introducing another option is to do with efficiency. All of the system software on the Edison is written in C and Linux is written in C. What this means is that C programs have a direct and uncomplicated connection to the system software. This makes C programs simpler and faster and if you are writing an application using embedded hardware then speed is usually an issue.

As well as speed, there is also the issue of timing. For many applications you have to be able to create a pulse of a known duration and within a specific time slot. The standard approach to Edison programming, i.e. using the Atom processor in Python say, isn't good enough for this task because there are too many overheads in running such a high level language.

If you use C and the techniques described in the following chapters then you stand a good chance of creating a program that is fast enough. Of course the Atom has only two cores which leaves only one core to do other things if your program is occupying the time of the other core. As long as one general purpose core is enough this is fine. If not you have little choice but to move to programming the second CPU on the Edison board, the MCU, which, at the moment, only be programmed in C. So if you want to future-proof your investment in the Edison, C has a lot going for it.

To summarize:

- C is fast, efficient and gets you close to the hardware

- You have to program the MCU in C so using it for the main processor as well makes sense.

Installing Eclipse

To write programs in C for the Edison the simplest way of working is to install and use the Eclipse IDE.

Eclipse is a well known IDE to Java programmers, but it is modular and can be customized to work with other languages. Intel has created a version of Eclipse specifically for the Edison, the Intel System Studio IoT Edition.

The advantage of using it is that it can be used to create C programs for the Edison and run and debug them very easily. You might outgrow the Eclipse approach, but it is very much the easiest way to get started.

If you use the Edison's Integrated Installer for Windows 64, Linux or OSX then one of the options is to install Eclipse. You can re-run the installer if you want to add Eclipse to your current setup or if you need to refresh it.

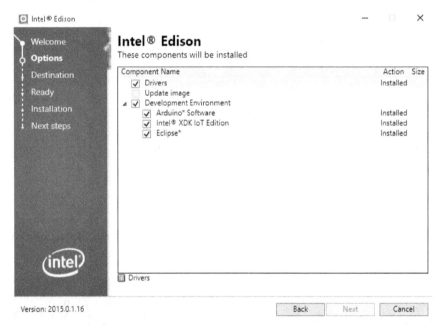

If there isn't an integrated installer for your OS then you can download Intel System Studio IoT Edition from the main IoT download site:

https://software.intel.com/iot/downloads

If you have to install manually you will need a copy of 7Zip for Windows and you will have to download, extract and run the installer. You also need a copy of the Java Runtime (JRE)because Eclipse is a Java program.

When you run Eclipse make sure you start it via the batch file:

```
devkit-launcher.bat -
```

This is what sets up the standard version of Eclipse to run the IoT extensions. If you start Eclipse by running Eclipse.exe then the IDE will start but you wont have the IoT extensions installed. The batch file is linked to via the Eclipse icons that the installer creates.

A First Project

When you first start Eclipse you will see the Intel IoT Developer Kit window. This is where you do everything that is specific to programming the Edison. If you need to see the IoT Developer Kit at any time just use the command Help,Intel IoT Developer Kit and the window will open. You can also pin the window as a sidebar in Eclipse so that you can see it all of the time.

A good place to start is the Hello World of IoT – blink an LED. In this case all we need to do is select:

```
Create C/C++ IoT project
```

and then select:

```
On board LED blink C
```

and call the project LED, or whatever you would like to call it.

At this point you might be a little puzzled as to what "On board LED" means. After all the mini-breakout board doesn't have an on board LED although the

29

Arduino breakout board does. Very few examples of using the mini-breakout board are included in the IDE, but this isn't a huge problem as we shall see.

Don't click Finish, instead click Next. You have to tell Eclipse how to connect to your Edison so that the program can be downloaded and run. All you have to do is enter the IP address of the Edison. If you have setup the WiFi then this connection will do the job perfectly, but there are other ways to connect an Edison to the Internet and these all work as well.

Enter the IP address, a name for the connection and a description if you want to:

At this point you could start programming, but it is worth checking that you do have a connection. This is also an opportunity to discover how to edit and make use of connections.

Remote Systems

At the bottom of the work areas you will see a Remote Systems tab. This is where the connections to the Edison and other machines are stored. If you click on the tab you should see the connection you created as part of the new project.

If you right-click on the Edison WiFi connection, you can select properties and edit its name, IP address, etc. One thing you often have to change is the Default User Id which generally defaults to the name of the host user rather than the Edison user:

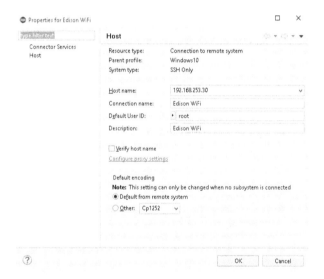

You can right click on any of the sub-items under the connection and select the connect option. You can use the Sftp connection to work with the Edison's file system.

To check that you have a connection the simplest thing to do is right click on the SSH terminals icon and select launch terminal. After you supply a password you should be able to use the terminal to work with Yocto Linux in the usual way.

```
Edison WiFi  ⊠
root@edison:~# ls
init_DIG.sh      init_i2c8.sh     otp.bin        set_DIG.sh
init_UART1.sh    init_mcu_PWM.sh  read_DIG.sh
root@edison:~# █
```

If you can't connect to the Edison via a terminal you won't be able to compile and run a program. So if it doesn't work you need to debug the connection before moving on. The only possibilities are that the Edison is setup for WiFi, you have the wrong IP address, or you didn't set a password and so SSH isn't enabled on all ports.

The Program

Now that we have a connection that works it is time to move to look at the program.

One of the big problems with using the Eclipse IDE is that the templates for the programs are limited, generally in C++ rather than C and specialized to the Arduino breakout board or some other device. For example, at the start of the template a test is made to see which device is being used. Of course as we are targeting the Edison with the mini-breakout board this is redundant code as far as we are concerned.

If you want to write C for the mini-breakout board then the simplest thing to do is use the LED C template, then delete most of the code and start afresh.

The key to programming the Edison's GPIO lines is the mraa library which is a low level interface to the hardware. When you run your project the IDE will check that the mraa library installed on the Edison it is connected to is up to date.

If you need to update the library manually all you have to do is copy and paste the following at the Linux command prompt:

1. echo "src maa-upm
   http://iotdk.intel.com/repos/1.1/intelgalactic" >
   /etc/opkg/intel-iotdk.conf
2. opkg update
3. opkg upgrade

The latest version of the IDE also checks to see if the libraries are up to date and will synchronize them if necessary.

We will look at the details of mraa in the next chapter, but for the moment all you need to know is that to use it you have to include its header file at the start of the program:

```
#include "mraa.h"
```

32

The steps in using mraa are fairly standard for the mini-breakout board. First you have to initialize the pin you want to use:

```
mraa_gpio_context pin = mraa_gpio_init(13);
```

We are using pin 13 and pin numbering is explained in detail later.

You can include an initialization of mraa if you want to, but strictly speaking it is unnecessary because the function is called when the module is loaded:

```
mraa_init();
```

We next need to set it to be an input or an output – an output in this case:

```
mraa_gpio_dir(pin, MRAA_GPIO_OUT);
```

Following this we can set it high using:

```
mraa_gpio_write(pin, 1);
```

and low using:

```
mraa_gpio_write(pin, 0);
```

Putting all this together the complete program we need to enter is:

```
#include "mraa.h"
#include <stdio.h>
#include <unistd.h>

int main()
{
 mraa_gpio_context pin = mraa_gpio_init(13);
 mraa_gpio_dir(pin, MRAA_GPIO_OUT);

 for (;;) {
  mraa_gpio_write(pin, 0);
  sleep(1);
  mraa_gpio_write(pin, 1);
  sleep(1);
 }

 return MRAA_SUCCESS;
}
```

The for loop for(;;){..} provides us with a simple C idiom for an infinite loop. The sleep(n) function delays execution for n seconds. Hence the program toggles pin 13 high and low every second.

As there is no LED connected to pin 13 you can test this using a multimeter, an oscilloscope or a logic analyzer.

GPIO line 13 is J17 pin 14 on the mini-breakout board:

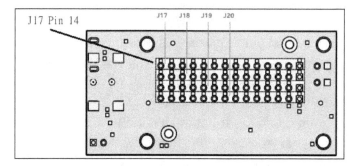

To run the program simply select the Run icon (green triangle) at the top of the work area, hit Ctrl-F11 or use the Run,Run menu item. The program will be compiled, downloaded to the Edison and run. You should see the voltage varying on the pin.

If you have a compilation error, check the program, correct the error and try again. If you have an error that says that the program couldn't be downloaded then the chances are that the Run configuration is using the wrong connection. Use the command Run,Run Configuration and make sure that the Connection field is showing the correct connection to the Edison – the one you tested in the previous section.

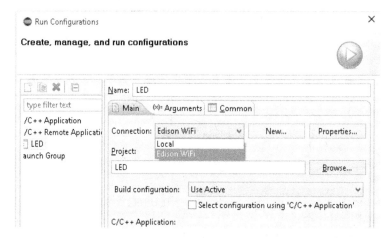

To check the running of the program you can select the Console tab at the bottom of the work area. You can use the red square icon to stop the program at any time.

The latest version of the IDE will automatically stop the previous running program if you try to run it again after making changes.

If something goes wrong and the program, in this case called LED, isn't stopped before a re-run then you will see an error message something like:

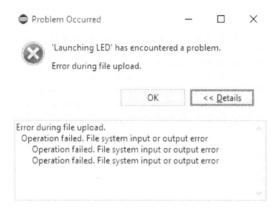

The solution to the problem is to launch a terminal: right-click on Ssh Terminal in the Remote Systems tab and select Launch. Switch to the terminal tab, i.e the terminal that you have just launched, and use the ps command to get a list of running processes:

```
 Problems  Tasks  Console  Properties  Terminals 23  Rem
 Edison WiFi 23
   678 root       0 SW   [kworker/0:2]
   680 root    5616 R    sshd: root@pts/0,pts/1
   682 root    2232 S    /usr/lib/openssh/sftp-serve
   683 root    2232 S    /usr/lib/openssh/sftp-serve
   687 root    3288 S    -sh
   689 root    2352 R    /tmp/LED
   690 root       0 SW   [kworker/0:1]
   691 root    3288 S    -sh
   692 root    2644 R    ps
```

Somewhere in the list will be a process corresponding to /tmp/LED, or more generally /tmp/projectname. Take note of the Process ID PID on the far left, 689 in this case, and enter the command:

```
kill 689
```

using the kill PID corresponding to your program.

This stops your program running and following this you can re-run it in the usual way.

Notice that what happens when you run a remote program is that Eclipse uploads the complied executable file to a the directory /tmp and then runs it. You can change the directory and file name that is used in the Run Configuration.

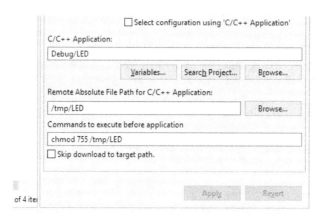

Also notice that you can enter commands to run before your program is run. In this case the chmod simply sets execute permission on the file so that it can be run.

Debugging

Debugging a realtime program is very difficult because generally you need to see it working at speed to see what is happening and pausing it often doesn't give you the information you need. However, Eclipse has a good debugging option and it works perfectly well with the Edison.

You can insert a breakpoint in the program simply by double clicking on the left margin next to an instruction. What is a breakpoint? It is a location in your program where, when run in debug mode, the program will a pause for you to examine the values stored in variables, etc.

For example to set a breakpoint on the line mraa_gpio_write(pin,0) you simply double-click in the margin and a round dot appears signifying a breakpoint:

To see the breakpoint in action you have to click the Debug icon, use the command Run,Debug or press F11. If you do this the layout of your workspace changes to show you additional debug windows. The program runs but pauses when it reaches the line with the breakpoint. In fact it stops before your breakpoint because it automatically breaks on the first line.

```
LED.c ☒   mraa.h      gpio.h      unistd.h      time.h

    #include "mraa.h"
    |
    #include <stdio.h>
    #include <unistd.h>

  int main() {
      mraa_gpio_context pin = mraa_gpio_init(13);
      mraa_gpio_dir(pin, MRAA_GPIO_OUT);
      for (;;) {
          mraa_gpio_write(pin, 0);
          sleep(1);
          mraa_gpio_write(pin, 1);
          sleep(1);
      }
      return MRAA_SUCCESS;
  }
```

To resume the program simply click the resume icon, use the command Run,Resume or press F8. This will allow the program to run to the first manually set breakpoint:

```
LED.c ☒   mraa.h      gpio.h      unistd.h      time.h

    #include "mraa.h"

    #include <stdio.h>
    #include <unistd.h>

  int main() {
      mraa_gpio_context pin = mraa_gpio_init(13);
      mraa_gpio_dir(pin, MRAA_GPIO_OUT);
      for (;;) {
          mraa_gpio_write(pin, 0);
          sleep(1);
          mraa_gpio_write(pin, 1);
          sleep(1);
      }
      return MRAA_SUCCESS;
  }
```

If you look at the variables window you will see that the pin variable is listed and it has a value shown in hexadecimal.

In a more complex program you can see all of the values of all of the variables and check that they are what you expected.

In the case of an internal value for an mraa_gpio_context we can see that the pin value isn't null and hence the mraa_gpio_init(13) worked.

You can explore the Run menu for all of the different ways you can resume and single-step through your program. They are all fairly obvious and you will soon be using the shortcuts to move through your program, checking what is happening at each step.

To return from the debug workspace to the standard programming workspace simply use the command:

```
Window, Open Perspective, C/C++
```

You can add and remove windows to customize a perspective to create a working environment that fits in with what you do most often.

Summary

1. C is the most direct and efficient way of working with the Edison's hardware. It isn't a difficult programming language and well worth learning.

2. Download and install Intel System Studio IoT Edition, the customized version of the Eclipse IDE provided for the Edison, which is a full function IDE complete with smart editor and debug facilities.

3. When you create a new project you have to create a connection to the Edison as a remote system. It is worth checking that you can connect via a terminal.

4. C programs, and programs in most other languages, make use of the mraa library and it is worth making sure it is up to date.

5. The Run,Configuration command lets you specify the remote system to download and run the program on among other things. If you can't get your program to run check that the remote system corresponding to your Edison is selected.

6. If you forget to stop your program before you start running it again, use a terminal to run the ps command and then kill the process that corresponds to your program.

7. You can debug your program simply by using the Run,Debug command.

8. Set breakpoints and use the variables window to confirm that what you think is happening is really happening.

The mraa library is designed to smooth out the differences between hardware. In this case hardware includes the breakout board you are using as well as the CPU.

The Edison with the Arduino breakout board is complicated because some of the raw pins are used for more than one thing – they are multiplexed – and there is a lot of extra hardware connected to the raw pins for analog I/O for example. Mraa provides a simple interface to this complicated mess and makes it look as if the Arduino "shield" I/O lines are simple GPIO lines.

The mini-breakout board simply delivers the raw I/O lines to the connectors with no processing of any kind. This makes the task of the mraa library much simpler. The mraa pin numbers map directly to physical pins on the connector and correspond to simple GPIO lines.

You can argue that the mraa library really only comes into its own when the breakout board needs to be configured as well as the raw GPIO lines, but as it already exists it is an easy and standard way to work with the native Edison hardware. However there is a problem that most of the documentation refers to the Arduino breakout board. This can be confusing. There are also times when the Arduino oriented software gets in the way of the "raw" approach of the mini-breakout board.

In this chapter we take a first look at using mraa to control the GPIO pins as basic input output lines in preparation for using low level protocols in C, i.e. bit-banging. It is worth noting that there is a C++ wrapping of the mraa library, but for simplicity only the C version will be used in this chapter. Switching to C++ is trivial.

If you know all about the basics of GPIO use including the subtleties of interrupt handling then jump to the next chapter.

Pin Numbering

One thing that drives Edison programmers crazy is the different pin numberings in use. Basically there are four different pin numberings – Arduino, mraa, SYSFS and, of course physical pin numbering. Of these the SYSFS number can be considered the "native" Edison GPIO numbering.

The Arduino pin numbering corresponds to standard Arduino shield pins. This is not in any way directly connected to the Edison GPIO numbering because multiple physical pins are used for different purposes on the Arduino breakout board.

If you use the mini-breakout or anything that is closer to the real Edison hardware you can mostly ignore Arduino pin numbering. The only time that it might be of concern is if you are trying to convert an Arduino sketch into C when you can look up which SYSFS number the pin corresponds to and then use the table given later to look up the corresponding mraa number.

The SYSFS pin numbers are the raw hardware defined GPIO lines that the Edison provides. In many ways you can consider these numbers to be reality. Linux exposes almost all external hardware as if it was a file system – character oriented like a terminal or block oriented like a disk. The GPIO lines are also provided to the user and programmer alike as a file system with each pin corresponding to an I/O stream. You can work directly with the GPIO by using Linux file commands and the pin numbering used is the standard hardware-derived numbering, see Chapter 16.

Finally we have the mraa numbering, which has nothing to do with anything as it is intended to provide a numbering that is independent of device and breakout board. Why this is an advantage is not entirely clear as most embedded programs target a specific platform and usually define things like pin numbers as constants at the start of the program. However, if you are going to use mraa, it is mraa's numbering you need to use.

You can see the pin numberings in the table below. Don't worry about Pinmode 1 for the moment. By default we are working with the I/O pins setup as Pinmode 0. In Pinmode 0 all of the lines are configured as digital I/O lines i.e. pure GPIO lines. In Pinmode 1 some of the pins have a special functions like PWM or I2C. In general you don't change the pinmode it is changed automatically when you select the special functions.

MRAA Number	Physical Pin	Edison Pin (SYSFS)	Pinmode 0	Pinmode1
0	J17-1	GP182	GPIO-182	PWM2
1	J17-2	NC		
2	J17-3	NC		
3	J17-4	VIN		
4	J17-5	GP135	GPIO-135	UART
5	J17-6	RCVR_MODE		
6	J17-7	GP27	GPIO-27	I2C-6-SCL
7	J17-8	GP20	GPIO-20	I2C-1-SDA
8	J17-9	GP28	GPIO-28	I2C-6-SDA
9	J17-10	GP111	GPIO-111	SPI-5-CS1
10	J17-11	GP109	GPIO-109	SPI-5-SCK
11	J17-12	GP115	GPIO-115	SPI-5-MOSI

12	J17-13	OSC_CLK_OUT_0		
13	J17-14	GP128	GPIO-128	UART-1-CTS
14	J18-1	GP13	GPIO-13	PWM1
15	J18-2	GP165	GPIO-165	
16	J18-3	GPI_PWRBTN_N		
17	J18-4	MSIC_SLP_CLK2		
18	J18-5	V_VBAT_BKUP		
19	J18-6	GP19	GPIO-19	I2C-1-SCL
20	J18-7	GP12	GPIO-12	PWM0
21	J18-8	GP183	GPIO-183	PWM3
22	J18-9	NC		
23	J18-10	GP110	GPIO-110	SPI-5-CS0
24	J18-11	GP114	GPIO-114	SPI-5-MISO
25	J18-12	GP129	GPIO-129	UART-1-RTS
26	J18-13	GP130	GPIO-130	UART-1-RX
27	J18-14	FW_RCVR		
28	J19-1	NC		
29	J19-2	V_V1P80		
30	J19-3	GND		
31	J19-4	GP44	GPIO-44	
32	J19-5	GP46	GPIO-46	
33	J19-6	GP48	GPIO-48	
34	J19-7	RESET_OUT		
35	J19-8	GP131	GPIO-131	UART-1-TX
36	J19-9	GP14	GPIO-14	
37	J19-10	GP40	GPIO-40	SSP2_CLK
38	J19-11	GP43	GPIO-43	SSP2_TXD
39	J19-12	GP77	GPIO-77	SD
40	J19-13	GP82	GPIO-82	SD
41	J19-14	GP83	GPIO-83	SD
42	J20-1	V_VSYS		
43	J20-2	V_V3P30		
44	J20-3	GP134		
45	J20-4	GP45	GPIO-45	
46	J20-5	GP47	GPIO-47	
47	J20-6	GP49	GPIO-49	
48	J20-7	GP15	GPIO-15	
49	J20-8	GP84	GPIO-84	SD
50	J20-9	GP42	GPIO-42	SSP2_RXD
51	J20-10	GP41	GPIO-41	SSP2_FS
52	J20-11	GP78	GPIO-78	SD
53	J20-12	GP79	GPIO-79	SD
54	J20-13	GP80	GPIO-80	SD
55	J20-14	GP81	GPIO-81	SD

You can see from the table that mraa line 13 which we toggled in the previous chapter is physically J17-14 and in Pinmode 0 is GPIO-128 as a SYSFS pin.

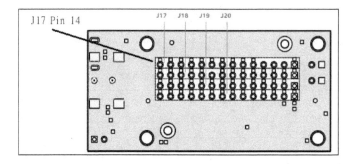

In most cases you can simply use the mraa pin number, but if you want to use the Edison Pin number which corresponds to the Linux SYSFS pin number you can via the mraa_gpio_init_raw function, which accepts SYSFS pin numbers. So you can change the init function to:

```
mraa_gpio_context pin = mraa_gpio_init_raw(128);
```

and still toggle the pin connected to J17-14.

The only reason for using SYSFS pin numbers is if you are converting a program written as a shell script.

Drive Characteristics

Each GPIO line can be configured as a general purpose I/O line.

For input the theoretical shortest pulse times that are recognized are given as:

- 100 ns for a 50 MHz clock when SoC is in S0 state.
- 260 ns for 19.2 MHz clock when SoC is in S0i1 or S0i2 State.
- 155.5 μs for 32 kHz clock (RTC) when SoC is in S0i3 State.

In most cases these smallest pulse widths are well below what can be measured using mraa.

In output mode each GPIO line can supply or sink 3mA – and this is an important number that you should keep in mind when designing interfaces.

Output

The mraa functions that you need to make use of a pin in output mode are very simple.

You need

```
mraa_gpio_init (mraa_pin)
mraa_gpio_init_raw (SYSFS_gpiopin)
```

To set the pin up using either mraa number or SYSFS number.

You also need:

```
mraa_gpio_dir (pin,dir)
```

to set the pin to output.

At its simplest, direction is 0 for output and 1 for input but there is an enumeration you can use:

```
MRAA_GPIO_OUT = 0
MRAA_GPIO_IN = 1
MRAA_GPIO_OUT_HIGH = 2
MRAA_GPIO_OUT_LOW = 3
```

The last two, dir=2 and dir=3 set the line to output and initially high or low if you need the line to be in a given state from the start.

The only other function that is specifically concerned with output is:

```
mraa_gpio_mode (pin, mode)
```

The output mode can be any of:

```
MRAA_GPIO_STRONG = 0
MRAA_GPIO_PULLUP = 1
MRAA_GPIO_PULLDOWN = 2
MRAA_GPIO_HIZ = 3
```

This works with the Arduino breakout board but not with the mini-breakout.

In the case of the mini-breakout board the default output mode is STRONG, i.e. pushpull, and you can't change this using mraa. However, you can change the output mode using SYSFS functions, see Chapter 16 for detailed information.

In particular, pullup mode is useful when you are working with devices that might also want to control the line. For example, if you select pullup mode then the Edison only drives the line low. When the line is set to high the drive is switched off and the line floats up to the high voltage (1.8V) via the resistor. If the device connected to the line pulls the line down in this mode it will go to 0V even though you have set the output to a high state.

This is, of course, how simple serial buses share a single data line.

For many direct drive applications, however, push-pull output is the correct choice.

Finally we have:

```
mraa_gpio_write (pin, value)
```

which sets the line to high or low

Note that all of these functions make use of the SYSFS method of working with the GPIO. That is, they are not interfacing directly with the GPIO driver.

Phased Pulses

As a simple example of using the mraa output functions let's write a short program that pulses two lines – one high and one low and then one low and one high, i.e. two pulse trains out of phase by 180 degrees.

The simplest program to do this job is:

```
#include "mraa.h"
#include <stdio.h>
#include <unistd.h>
int main()
{
 mraa_init();
 mraa_gpio_context pin15 = mraa_gpio_init(15);
 mraa_gpio_dir(pin15, MRAA_GPIO_OUT_HIGH);
 mraa_gpio_context pin31 = mraa_gpio_init(31);
 mraa_gpio_dir(pin31, MRAA_GPIO_OUT_LOW);
 for (;;) {
  mraa_gpio_write(pin15, 0);
  mraa_gpio_write(pin31, 1);
  mraa_gpio_write(pin15, 1);
  mraa_gpio_write(pin31, 0);
 }
 return MRAA_SUCCESS;
}
```

Notice that there is no delay in the loop so the pulses are produced at the fastest possible speed. Mraa pin 15 is J18-2 and 31 is J19-4. Ground is J19-3. The intent is for both actions to occur at the same time, but using a logic analyzer reveals that the result isn't what you might expect:

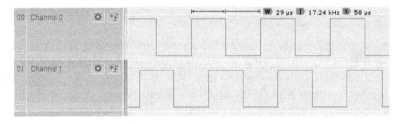

44

You can see that the pulse trains are not 180 degrees out of phase. The top train switches on but the bottom train takes about half a pulse before it switches off. The point is that it does take quite a long time to access and change the state of an output line.

Of course, if we include a delay to increase the pulse width then the delay caused by accessing the pin via SYSFS is a smaller proportion of the total and the lag isn't so important:

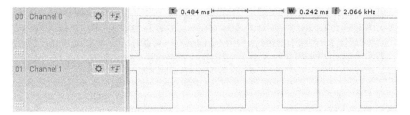

In this case the loop now has usleep(100) delays, i.e. 100 microsecond pauses:

```
for (;;) {
mraa_gpio_write(pin15, 0);
mraa_gpio_write(pin31, 1);
usleep(100);
mraa_gpio_write(pin15, 1);
mraa_gpio_write(pin31, 0);
usleep(100);
}
```

You will notice that the pulses are now nearly 500 microseconds wide and they are changing at what looks like nearer to being the same time.

The point is that when you call usleep(100) you yield the thread to the operating system which might well schedule another thread to run – so you usually get a delay that is longer than 100 microseconds. More about how to get around this sort of problem is in the next chapter.

There is still a lag, but in many applications it might not be important. In other applications it could be crucial. For example, if the two pulse trains were driving different halves of a motor controller bridge there would be a significant time when both were high – so shorting the power supply. It might only be for 10 microseconds, but over time it could well damage the power supply. Of course, any sensible, cautious, engineer wouldn't feed a motor control bridge from two independently generated pulse trains unless they were guaranteed not to switch both sides of the bridge on at the same time. That is, a bridge circuit should be driven with a pair of non-overlap on pulse trains.

There are ways of improving on this situation because most of the delays are due to mraa having to make use of SYSFS which is slow – see the next chapter.

Basic Input

Reading the state of an input line 0 or 1.8V is easy. You set the direction to input and then make use of:

```
mraa_gpio_read (pin)
```

which returns a 0 if the input is 0 and 1 if it is 1.8V. Simple, but in most cases input isn't that easy for reasons that have to do with timing.

The most common use case for input is just reading the state of a switch – open or closed. In other words, the input line is either high or low according to the relatively slow change of state of the switch. You can read the state of such a slow changing line using polling – i.e. a loop that reads the input over and over:

```c
#include "mraa.h"
#include <stdio.h>
#include <unistd.h>

int main()
{

 mraa_init();
 mraa_gpio_context pin31 = mraa_gpio_init(31);
 mraa_gpio_dir(pin31, MRAA_GPIO_IN);
 int in;
 for (;;) {
  in=mraa_gpio_read(pin31);
  printf("switch %d \n",in);
  usleep(1000*1000);
 }
 return MRAA_SUCCESS;
}
```

This reads the state of the line every second, usleep(n) pauses for n microseconds, and prints the result to the Eclipse console. If you connect the input line J19-4 to 1.8V J19-2 or to 0V J19-3 then you will see the output change to 1 and back to 0.

In practice you also need a way to debounce the switch. This can be done using a delay between reading the switch or you can use the well known integration method – read the switch n times and sum the result and use a threshold to determine if the state is on or off.

Notice that if you speed up the polling loop to take readings more often there will come a point where the printf is the limiting factor.

If you want to use a switch to do the job then you need a circuit something like:

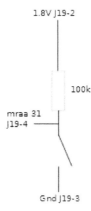

Polling for input is a problem in that it often means that your program is tied up doing nothing but polling. This doesn't mean that the operating system won't suspend your program, run something else and then restart your program. Even with polling you cannot guarantee to respond to a change in an input line within a given time.

The big problem with polling is that your program can't get on with doing anything else. Sometimes this doesn't matter because you need input as fast as possible for a short time. Sometimes it does matter and when it does the solution is to use an interrupt.

Interrupts

If you know another programming language then you can think of an interrupt as an event and an interrupt handler as an event handler. In this case, however, an interrupt is caused by an external event – like an input line changing its value. When the interrupt occurs your specified interrupt handler is called. You can also set what actually constitutes an event - the input can be edge-triggered from low to high or from high to low or both. There is a predefined enumeration you can use:

```
MRAA_GPIO_EDGE_NONE = 0,
MRAA_GPIO_EDGE_BOTH = 1,
MRAA_GPIO_EDGE_RISING = 2,
MRAA_GPIO_EDGE_FALLING = 3
```

To set an interrupt handler you use the function:

```
mraa_gpio_isr(pin,edge,pointerToFunction,pointerToArgs)
```

The first parameter determines the pin and the second determines what causes the interrupt. The final parameters determine the function called when the interrupt happened and a parameter to pass to the function.

You can also use

```
mraa_gpio_isr_exit(pin)
```

to remove the interrupt handler associated with a pin.

The simplest example of interrupt input is:

```
#include "mraa.h"
#include <stdio.h>
#include <unistd.h>

void switchChange();

int main(){
 mraa_init();
 mraa_gpio_context pin31 = mraa_gpio_init(31);
 mraa_gpio_dir(pin31, MRAA_GPIO_IN);
 mraa_gpio_isr(pin31, MRAA_GPIO_EDGE_FALLING, &switchChange,NULL);
 for (;;) {};

 return MRAA_SUCCESS;
}

void switchChange(){
 printf("switch \n");
}
```

You can see that the main program doesn't actually do anything once it has setup the input pin and interrupts - it just loops forever. After initializing pin 31 and setting it to input, an interrupt triggered on the falling edge of the input is set. Notice that for simplicity the final parameters, args, isn't used in this example - it is set to a NULL pointer.

The interrupt handler just prints the fact that the switch has been pressed, i.e. a falling edge. If you run this program you should see "switch" printed in the Eclipse Console each time the switch is pressed. When the switch is released it generates a rising edge and you can generate an interrupt on both edges using:

```
MRAA_GPIO_EDGE_BOTH
```

We can use the arg parameter to pass in the details of the pin that caused the interrupt and allow the interrupt handler to read the state of the pin:

```
#include "mraa.h"
#include <stdio.h>
#include <unistd.h>

void switchChange(void* pin);
int main(){
 mraa_init();
 mraa_gpio_context pin31 = mraa_gpio_init(31);
 mraa_gpio_dir(pin31, MRAA_GPIO_IN);
 mraa_gpio_isr(pin31, MRAA_GPIO_EDGE_BOTH,
                          &switchChange,pin31);
 for (;;) {};
 return MRAA_SUCCESS;
}

void switchChange(void* pin){
    int s=mraa_gpio_read((mraa_gpio_context) pin);
    printf("switch %d \n",s);
}
```

Notice that way that arg parameter is passed as a pointer to void - a C idiom for passing a pointer to any data type. Also notice that we don't have to dereference pin because mraa_gpio_context is already a pointer to struct and the dereference is automatic.

When you run this program you will see the switch state printed each time it changes, i.e. when the switch is pressed and released.

In general it is preferable to use an interrupt to service changes in input state unless you have a very specific reason not to – and the most common reason is that you need to work with very fast changes in the input.

How Edison Interrupts Work

If you know something about interrupts in other systems you will probably be very pleased that the Edison provides a per pin interrupt system. However things are not quite what they seem. The pin interrupts are not true interrupts but software simulated interrupts.

What happens when you set an interrupt on a pin is that mraa creates a new thread and starts makes a blocking call to the Linux system call poll. This only returns when there is an event in the SYSFS file system for the file corresponding to the pin you have attached the interrupt handler to. There are a number of consequences of this implementation.

The first is that the response time isn't a fast as you might expect a hardware based interrupt to be. The polling loop is run on new thread and this is scheduled by Linux in the usual way, meaning that it could take milliseconds in the worst case to respond to a change.

The second is that if the event occurs during the call to poll your interrupt handler is called on the thread and this naturally stops any additional interrupts occurring. That is you cannot have the same interrupt during the execution of an interrupt handler – the interrupt is automatically disabled.

The third is that because mraa will only spin up a single thread for each pin and, because SYSFS doesn't tell mraa what edge transition occurred, you can only associate one interrupt handler per pin.

Also when the interrupt handler is called it is running on a different thread to the main program. This means you cannot use mraa_gpio_isr_exit (pin) to remove an interrupt handler from within the interrupt handler, something that would be possible with a real interrupt. The reason is simply that the isr_exit function stops the thread that is running the interrupt and must be run on the main function's thread. The inability to change interrupt handler after an interrupt means you cannot set up a chain of handlers that deal with a rising edge, then a falling edge.

It also means that the parameter you pass to the interrupt handler has to be accessible from another thread and any variable created in the interrupt handler belong to the interrupt thread.

Pulse Width Measurement

Let's finish with an example of measuring a pulse width as this is a common task. In this case the pulse will be generated by a switch as in the last example, but in general the pulse could come from almost anything.

Assume that a falling edge triggers the start of the measurement and a rising edge ends the interval. If we were working with physical interrupts we could try something clever like setting one interrupt handler for the rising edge and another for the falling edge. As only one interrupt handler can be set per pin this isn't possible. Equally we can't set a falling edge interrupt which, when it is called sets a rising edge interrupt handler, because you can't change an interrupt handler from within an interrupt handler.

The only way to make this work is to set up a single interrupt handler that is to set up an interrupt handler for both edge transitions and read the pin to find out which one is occurring. On the falling edge you read the system clock and store the value. On the rising edge you read the system clock again and work out the difference between the two values.

This is quite simple. In the main program we have:

```
mraa_init();
mraa_gpio_context pin31 = mraa_gpio_init(31);
mraa_gpio_dir(pin31, MRAA_GPIO_IN);
mraa_gpio_isr(pin31, MRAA_GPIO_EDGE_BOTH,
                     &switchPressed, pin31);
for (;;) {};
```

The interrupt handler is a little more complicated. First we get the time that the interrupt handler was entered:

```
void switchPressed(void* pin) {
 struct timespec ttime;
 clock_gettime(CLOCK_REALTIME, &ttime);
```

Next we read the pin to discover what transition has occurred and either save the start time or compute the interval:

```
int s = mraa_gpio_read((mraa_gpio_context) pin);
if (s == 0) {
 btime=ttime;
}
else
{
 double nseconds = (double)((ttime.tv_sec-btime.tv_sec)
  *BILLION)+(double)(ttime.tv_nsec-btime.tv_nsec );
  printf("time = %f (s)  \n ", nseconds/BILLION);}
}
```

Notice that while clock_gettime returns a structure with seconds and nanoseconds the time isn't accurate to the nearest nanosecond.

If you run this program you will discover that it sort of works. Occasionally it will get a negative time because a rising edge occurs before a falling edge. If you are using a mechanical switch to generate the pulses you will also discover that you get multiple pulses for each press of the switch. The reason for this is switch bounce. When you press a switch it doesn't make contact cleanly – the voltage goes up and down until it settles at the low - and when you release the switch the bounce generates multiple rising edges. The slowness of the interrupt means that you are unlikely to see many pulses due to switch bounce but in the real work you will have to debounce the switch either physically or in the software.

To physically debounce a switch you add a capacitor, but software debounce is very easy – simply add a delay before reading the pin's state to give it time to settle. The only problem is how long to wait? For the switch used here, and for most switches, a usleep(500), i.e. half a millisecond wait, should be enough. Note that in practice the wait is likely to be longer than 500 microseconds because of Linux task scheduling.

The complete program, including debounce, is:

```c
#include "mraa.h"
#include <stdio.h>
#include <unistd.h>
#include <time>

#define BILLION 1000000000L
struct timespec btime, etime;__time_t i;

void switchPressed(void* pin);

int main()
{
 mraa_init();
 mraa_gpio_context pin31 = mraa_gpio_init(31);
 mraa_gpio_dir(pin31, MRAA_GPIO_IN);
 mraa_gpio_isr(pin31, MRAA_GPIO_EDGE_BOTH,
                         &switchPressed, pin31);
 for (;;) {};
 return MRAA_SUCCESS;
}

void switchPressed(void* pin) {
 struct timespec ttime;
 clock_gettime(CLOCK_REALTIME, &ttime);
 usleep(500);
 int s = mraa_gpio_read((mraa_gpio_context) pin);
 if (s == 0)
 {
   btime=ttime;
 }
 else
 {
   double nseconds = (double)(
     (ttime.tv_sec-btime.tv_sec)*BILLION)+
     (double)(ttime.tv_nsec-btime.tv_nsec ) ;
   printf("time = %f (s)  \n ", nseconds/BILLION);
 }
}
```

Summary

1. Intel Edison pin numberings can be confusing. You can mostly ignore Arduino pin numbering when working with the mini-breakout board. Use mraa pin numbers or SYSFS GPIO numbers.

2. To initialize a pin use either:
    ```
    mraa_gpio_init (mraa_pin)
    mraa_gpio_init_raw (SYSFS_gpiopin)
    ```

3. Set the direction of the pin with:
    ```
    mraa_gpio_dir (pin,dir)
    ```

4. Set the mode if you need to with:
    ```
    mraa_gpio_mode (pin, mode)
    ```
    This only works with the Arduino board. The default for the mini board is STRONG or pushpull mode. This cannot be changed using mraa.

5. For output write a 0 or a 1 using:
    ```
    mraa_gpio_write (pin, value)
    ```

6. Mraa uses SYSFS to control the state of a GPIO line. This, and the fact that Linux can suspend the operation of your program at any time, means that you cannot rely on how fast you can change an I/O line. In particular, if you set multiple lines don't expect the change to happen at the same time.

7. For input use:
    ```
    mraa_gpio_read (pin)
    ```

8. You can either read the state of a GPIO line using a polling loop or you can use an interrupt.

9. To associate a function with an interrupt use:
    ```
    mraa_gpio_isr(pin,edge,pointerToFunction,pointerToArgs)
    ```

10. It is important to know that Edison interrupts are not hardware interrupts but software simulated interrupts. What happens is that when you associate an interrupt function with a pin event a new thread is created which polls the pin until the event occurs when it then calls your function. The interrupt system makes use of SYSFS for all pin interactions.

11. Software simulated interrupts have a number of drawbacks. You can only have a single interrupt handler per pin. You cannot change or remove and interrupt handler within an interrupt handler. Most importantly, the interrupt handler thread is scheduled by Linux in the usual way and as such you cannot rely on a speedy or timely response.

12. If you need the fastest response time then use a polling loop and some or all of the techniques discussed in the next chapter.

Chapter 5

Fast Memory Mapped I/O

In the previous chapter we learned how to make use of the GPIO as simple input and output. The biggest problem we encountered was that everything was on the slow side. Fast memory mapped mode allows the Edison to generate pulses as short as 0.25 microseconds wide and to work with input pulses in the 10-microsecond region.

There are many applications where the speed of the GPIO doesn't matter because slow in this case means around 100 microseconds to 1 millisecond. Many applications work in near human time and the Edison is plenty fast enough just using standard mraa calls or SYSFS.

However, there are applications where response times in the microsecond range are essential. For example the well know art of "bit-banging" where you write a program to use the I/O lines to implement some communications protocol.

While the Edison has support for I2C, for example, it lacks native support for alternatives such as the 1-wire bus and custom protocols such as that use with the very useful and popular DHT11 and DHT22 temperature and humidity sensors. In such cases speed is essential if it is going to be possible to write a bit-banging interface.

There is also a second issue involved in using the Edison for time critical operations. The fastest pulse you can produce or read depends on the speed of the processor and, as we will see, the Edison's Atom processor is fast enough to generate pulses at the 1 microsecond level. (At the time of writing this seems to be faster than the MCU can work although this might improve with new releases of the SDK.)

Another problem is caused by the fact that Linux is not a realtime operating system. Linux runs many processes and threads at the same time by allocating each one a small time slice in turn. That is all of the processes that you can see in the process queue (use the ps, command to see a list) each get their turn to run.

What this means is that your program could be suspended at any time and it could be suspended for milliseconds. If your program is performing a bit-banging operation the entire exchange could be brought to a halt by another process that is given the CPU for its time slice. This would cause the protocol to be broken and the only option would be to start over and hope that the transaction could be completed.

It is generally stated, often with absolute certainty, that you cannot do realtime, and bit-banging in particular under a standard Linux OS, which is what Yocto Linux is. This is true but you can do near realtime on any Linux distribution based on the 2.6 kernel or later, i.e. most versions including the current Yocto. This is easier than you might imagine but there are some subtle problems that you need to know about.

In this chapter we tackle the problem of speed both output and input. In the next chapter we tackle smoothing out the glitches using the Linux scheduler.

How Fast?

Before looking at speeding things up let's have a look at how good the current mraa read/write routines are. First we need to know how fast can you toggle the I/O lines?

If you write a loop which does nothing but change the line:

```
for (;;) {
 mraa_gpio_write(pin, 0);
 mraa_gpio_write(pin, 1);
}
```

the line is switched as fast as the software can manage it.

In this case the pulse width is about 15 microseconds.

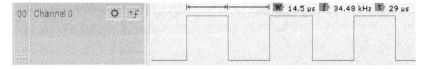

This is reasonable, but notice that this is running under a general purpose Linux and every now and again the program will be suspended while the operating system does something else. In other words, you can generate a 15 microsecond pulse but you can't promise exactly when this will occur.

Using a different scale on the logic analyzer, it is fairly easy to find one or more irregularities:

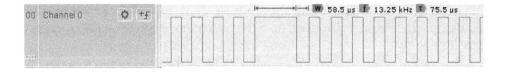

So on this occasion the generated pulse was roughly four times the length of the usual pulse. This is typical for a lightly loaded system, but it can be much worse.

How do we go about creating a pulse of a given length? There are two general methods. You can use a function that sleeps the thread for a specified time, or you can use a busy wait, i.e. a loop that keeps the thread and just wastes some time looping.

Delay Using usleep

The simplest way of sleeping a thread for a number of microseconds is to use usleep. To try this, include a call to usleep(10) to delay the pulse:

```
for (;;) {
  mraa_gpio_write(pin, 0);
  usleep(10);
  mraa_gpio_write(pin, 1);
  usleep(10);
}
```

You will discover that adding usleep(10) doesn't increase the pulse length by 10 microseconds but by just over 100 microseconds. You will also discover that the glitches have gone and most of the pulses are about 130 microseconds long.

What seems to be happening is that calling usleep yields the thread to the operating system and this incurs an additional 50 microsecond penalty due to calling the scheduler. There are also losses that are dependent on the time you set to wait – usleep only promises that your thread will not restart for **at least** the specified time.

If you look at how the delay time relates to the average pulse length things seem complicated:

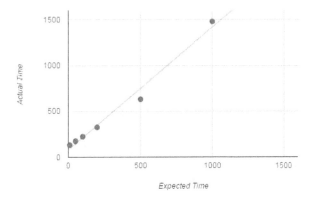

You can see that there is about a 78 microsecond fixed overhead but you also get a delay of roughly 1.34 microseconds for each microsecond you specify. If you want a pulse of length t microseconds then use a delay given by:

```
t'= t * 0.74 - 57
```

Notice that this only accurate to tens of microseconds over the range 100 to 1000 microseconds.

Busy wait

The problem with usleep is that it hands the thread over to the operating system which then runs another thread and returns control to your thread only when it is ready to. This works and it smooths out the glitches we saw in the loop without usleep – because usleep yields to the operating system there is no need for it to preempt your thread at other times.

An alternative to usleep or any function that yields control to the operating system is to busy wait. In this case your thread stays running on the CPU but the operating system will preempt it and run some other thread. Surprisingly a simple null for loop works very well as a busy wait;

```
int i;
for (;;) {
 mraa_gpio_write(pin31, 0);
 for(i=0;i<100;i++){};
 mraa_gpio_write(pin31, 1);
 for(i=0;i<100;i++){};
}
```

If you try this out you will discover that you can calibrate the number of loops per microsecond delay produced. If you want to produce a pulse of duration t microseconds the number of loops to use is:

```
n = 62.113 * t - 912.45
```

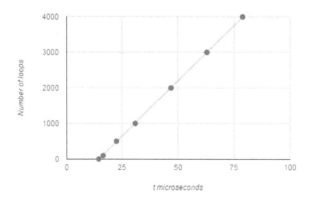

For example to create a 100 microsecond pulse you need:

$$62.113*100-912.45 = 5299 \text{ loops.}$$

```
int i;
for (;;) {
 mraa_gpio_write(pin31, 0);
 for(i=0;i<5299;i++){};
 mraa_gpio_write(pin31, 1);
 for(i=0;i<5299;i++){};
}
```

This produces pulses that are close to 100 microseconds, roughly in the range 89 to 108 microseconds – but the glitches are back:

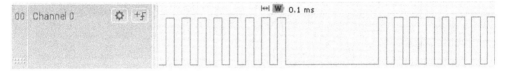

We now have pauses in the pulse train that are often 1100 microseconds and very occasionally more. This should not be surprising. We are now keeping the thread for the full amount of time the operating system allows until it preempts our program and runs or contemplates running another thread.

At the moment it looks like busy waiting is a good plan, but it has problems. The most obvious is that you have to rely on the time to perform one loop not changing. This is something that worries most programmers, but if you are targeting a particular CPU there isn't much that happens to change the speed of a for loop. If you are worried about what happens if the Edison is upgraded to a faster clock then you could put a calibration stage in at the start of your program and time how long 5000 loops take and then compute the necessary busy wait parameters for the time periods your program uses.

The idea of calibration seems like a good one but it isn't going to be foolproof unless we can find a way to stop the glitches caused by the operating system's scheduler putting arbitrary delays into our program anytime it needs to run another thread. More on this in the next chapter.

Fast Mapped I/O

The most recent versions of mraa support another way to access the GPIO and it is much faster.

Most of the delay in setting the GPIO line is due to mraa using the Linux SYSFS subsystem. SYSFS is a file system that can be used for all sorts of interfacing tasks. In this case SYSFS is being used to map the GPIO pins as if they were files in a file system. This has the advantage of making the GPIO available to almost anything that runs under Linux, but has the disadvantage of a high overhead.

A faster way to work with the GPIO lines is to allow the software to write directly to the memory locations where the GPIO port registers live. This is a standard part of the SYSFS facility and there is a special file that memory maps the driver so writing to a particular address sets a given line high and to another address sets it low.

Notice that using memory mapped I/O only changes the way the line is read or written. For all other operations such as setting the line's direction a SYSFS call is used.

The installation of the memory map is something mraa can do and it will substitute memory mapped read and write function for any given pin. The addresses and data masks are computed from scratch each time and there is a slight speed up to be gained by precomputing them and providing your own read/write functions for each pin. However the gains are hardly worth it as we will soon discover.

You can set how any pin is accessed using the function:

```
mraa_gpio_use_mmaped(pin,1/0)
```

If the second parameter is 1 then the pin is accessed directly i.e. a fast memory mapped access. If the parameter is 0 the slower SYSFS interface is used. Changing the program to use fast I/O on pin 31:

```
#include "mraa.h"
#include <stdio.h>
#include <unistd.h>

int main()
{
 mraa_gpio_context pin31=mraa_gpio_init(31);
 mraa_gpio_dir(pin31, MRAA_GPIO_OUT);
 mraa_gpio_use_mmaped(pin31,1);
 for (;;) {
  mraa_gpio_write(pin31, 0);
  mraa_gpio_write(pin31, 1);
 }
 return MRAA_SUCCESS;
}
```

With this change the line is toggled for approximately 0.25 microsecond high and 0.3 microseconds low which is around 60 times faster. The reason for the difference in the high and low times is that at this frequency capacitive effects become important and the wave form isn't a perfect square wave. The exact timing figures you get will depend on the logic thresholds used by the measuring device.

Putting this another way the SYSFS approach can produce a 0.03 Mhz pulse train but memory mapping can produce a (close to) 2Mhz pulse train. Of course we still have the problem that the program is running under a non-real-time operating system and therefore it will be interrupted and there will be jitter in the faster pulse train as well. The next step is to create pulses longer than 0.25 microseconds.

There isn't much point in trying to use usleep because the overhead in yielding to the operating system is such that usleep(1) produces 98 microsecond pulse. In other words using usleep with fast memory map access produces pulses in the same sort of region as you can create using slow SYSFS.

If you want to use usleep with fast memory mapped mraa you can use the following formula to work out the delay.

If you want a pulse of width t microseconds delay in usleep for :

```
t' = 0.999*t - 92.5
```

This is accurate from 100 to 800 microseconds.

If you want to generate pulses in the range 0.25 to 100 microsecond range then you have little option but to busy wait.

```c
#include "mraa.h"
#include <stdio.h>
#include <unistd.h>

int main()
{
 mraa_gpio_context pin31=mraa_gpio_init(31);
 mraa_gpio_dir(pin31, MRAA_GPIO_OUT);
 mraa_gpio_use_mmaped(pin31,1);
 int i;
 for (;;) {
  mraa_gpio_write(pin31, 0);
  for(i=1;i<7500;i++){};
  mraa_gpio_write(pin31, 1);
  for(i=1;i<7500;i++){};
 }
 return MRAA_SUCCESS;
}
```

The relationship between loop counter and pulse length is linear up to at least 100 microseconds.

The formula for the number of loops needed to create a pulse of length t is:

```
n = 71.36*t - 21.276
```

So for a 10 microsecond pulse you need 692 loops. Not perfect, but a good start for manual trimming.

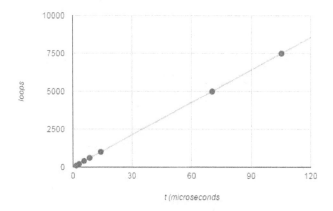

t (microseconds

In short using fast memory mapped output and busy wait you can generate reasonably accurate 1 to 10 microsecond pulses.

Notice that this doesn't mean we are home and dry when it comes to fast output. If you try to change multiple lines within a loop then the time for each loop increases and there will be phase shifts between the pulses generated.

For example:

```
#include <stdio.h>
#include <unistd.h>
int main(){
 mraa_init();
 mraa_gpio_context pin15 = mraa_gpio_init(15);
 mraa_gpio_dir(pin15, MRAA_GPIO_OUT_HIGH);
 mraa_gpio_use_mmaped(pin15,1);
 mraa_gpio_context pin31 = mraa_gpio_init(31);
 mraa_gpio_dir(pin31, MRAA_GPIO_OUT_LOW);
 mraa_gpio_use_mmaped(pin31,1);
 for (;;) {
  mraa_gpio_write(pin15, 0);
  mraa_gpio_write(pin31, 1);
  mraa_gpio_write(pin15, 1);
  mraa_gpio_write(pin31, 0);
 }
 return MRAA_SUCCESS;
}
```

This is the two-pulse train generator given in the previous chapter now speeded up using memory mapped output. The pulse length increases to 0.5 microseconds, i.e. double, and you still have the same order or phase shift between the two pulse trains:

Notice however that each pulse is 0.5 microseconds and the overlap is for a much shorter time, approximately 0.25 microsecond.

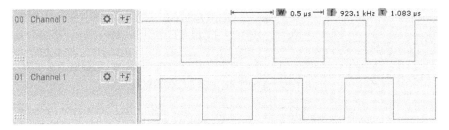

However the comparison isn't completely fair. If you generate memory mapped pulses of the same sort of length as the SYSFS approach works with then things look a lot better:

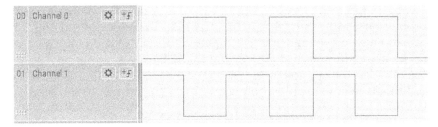

Now it does look as if the pulse trains are out of phase and the overlap is smaller. The point is that memory mapping is not just for short pulse durations but for more accurate pulse generation. Without a register based access to the GPIO which would allow you to set multiple pinouts in one operation this is about as good as it gets.

Fast Input

Now we have to try to answer the question of how fast a pulse Edison can measure on input.

Input is more difficult to quantify because you have to take potentially many measurements to track an input pulse. There is no point in trying to use an interrupt approach because interrupts always make use of SYSFS and this is slow. If you want the advantages of memory mapped I/O you have to use a polling loop.

A simple measurement of how long it takes to perform multiple reads from a single input line gives a reasonable estimate of how fast input can be.

- Using SYSFS you can read the line 100 times in about 1300 microseconds, which is made up of about a 250 microsecond overhead and 10 microseconds per sample.

- Using memory mapped input you can read 100 times in about 70 microseconds made up of about 11 microseconds overhead and 0.68 microseconds per sample.

With these estimates it should be possible to read in pulse trains consisting of 10 microsecond pulses using memory mapped input and 100 microsecond pulses using SYSFS. Putting this another way for a 10 microsecond pulse memory mapped input should allow you to get 15 samples per pulse allowing you to time it with an accuracy of about 0.5 microseconds.

There are two ways of reading data even using a polling loop. You can opt to use the system to time how long an input hasn't changed with something like:

```
clock_gettime(CLOCK_REALTIME, &btime);
for(;;){
 if(mraa_gpio_read(pin31)==0)break;
}
clock_gettime(CLOCK_REALTIME, &ttime);
```

The problem with this approach is that the real-time clock might claim to be accurate to nanosecond, but it isn't. In fact, on the Edison it is too coarse to be used to measure the smallest pulses that the Edison is capable of. There is also the fact that the call to clock_gettime takes around 4 microseconds per call and this is a lot to spend when you are working at the 10 microsecond region.

A much better idea is to simply use a busy wait implemented as a for loop and use the value of the index when the loop is exited as a measure of time. Use something like:

```
for(i=0;i<10000;i++){
 if(mraa_gpio_read(pin31)==0)break;
}
```

This also has the advantage that the value that you set for the maximum number of loops, i.e. 10,000 in this example, acts as a timeout. The value of i when the loop exits gives you a measure of how long the line was low for.

Using this simple construction we can easily write a program that measures the length of a high pulse. This is a tiny bit more complicated than you might expect because we only want to measure a single pulse in a uniform pulse train.

The algorithm is to first wait for the line to go low. Then wait for it to go high and then wait for it to go low keeping the count of the number of times the loop iterated.

That is, wait for the line to go low:

```
for(;;){
 if(mraa_gpio_read(pin31)==0)break;
}
```

Next wait for the line to go high:

```
for(i=0;i<10000;i++){
  if(mraa_gpio_read(pin31)==1)break;
}
```

Finally wait for the line to go low again:

```
for(i=1;i<10000;i++){
  if(mraa_gpio_read(pin31)==0)break;
}
```

The width of the pulse is given by the value of i when the final loop exits. Notice that the count in the final loop starts from 1 because we can count the single high sample that ended the second loop as the first high measurement.

The complete program to measure a single pulse and display the "time" in the Eclipse console is:

```
#include <stdio.h>
#include <unistd.h>

int main() {
 mraa_init();
 mraa_gpio_context pin31 = mraa_gpio_init(31);
 mraa_gpio_dir(pin31, MRAA_GPIO_IN);
 mraa_gpio_use_mmaped(pin31,1);
 int i;

 for(;;){
  if(mraa_gpio_read(pin31)==0)break;
 }

 for(i=0;i<10000;i++){
  if(mraa_gpio_read(pin31)==1)break;
 }

 for(i=1;i<10000;i++){
  if(mraa_gpio_read(pin31)==0)break;
 }

 printf("%d \n",i);
 return MRAA_SUCCESS;
}
```

If you feed a range of pulse widths into the input line you can obtain a calibration chart.

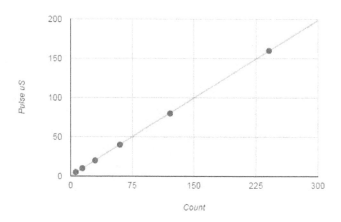

You can use the approximate formula:

```
t = 0.66 * i + 0.548 microseconds
```

to convert from final loop count to time in microseconds.

This means that if you are trying to measure a 5-microsecond pulse you can expect to get six samples while it is high giving an accuracy of something like 1 microsecond. The number of samples for various sizes of pulse are:

Pulse uS	Samples
5	6
10	14
20	30
40	60
80	121
160	241

Getting 6 samples per pulse isn't great but it is enough to tell the difference between a 5 and 10 microsecond pulse. Notice also that you can't afford to do any computation in the measuring loop otherwise you will reduce the sampling rate. If you are measuring the time the pulse is high there is usually more time to do things in the low part of the pulse because you don't care as much exactly when you start the polling loop, as long as it is before the pulse goes high again.

Direct Memory Mapping

It was mentioned earlier that it was possible to by-pass mraa and write to the GPIO directly – surely this must be faster? To avoid you wasting time on this question here is a program that works directly with the in memory driver – and it is no faster than going via mraa. This is a puzzle.

Rather than modifying mraa to get the information we need to locate the memory mapped driver, it is easier to create a function that loads the driver:

```
uint8_t* load_memmap(){
```

```
 int mmap_fd;
 struct stat fd_stat;
 uint8_t* mmap_reg;
 mmap_fd = open(
 "/sys/devices/pci0000:00/0000:00:0c.0/resource0",
    O_RDWR);
 fstat(mmap_fd, &fd_stat);
 mmap_reg =(uint8_t*) mmap(NULL, fd_stat.st_size,
    PROT_READ | PROT_WRITE, MAP_FILE | MAP_SHARED,
    mmap_fd, 0);
 return mmap_reg;
}
```

This function is essentially a modified version of how mraa loads the driver. The driver is a file in /sys/devices which is opened and then loaded using the mmap function. The function returns mmap_reg, which gives the location of the driver in memory. This is essentially what a call to

```
    mraa_gpio_use_mmaped
```

does the first time you call it.

As always, to make the logic clear, no error detection code has been included. The most likely error is that the file is missing or has changed its name due to an update. Now we have the driver loaded into memory we have to work out various addresses and two masks. The address we need depends on the pin number:

```
    uint8_t*  loc=(pin / 32) * sizeof(uint32_t)+ mmap_reg;
```

This gives the start address of the area that controls the pin – note that the pin number is the SYSFS pin number not the mraa number. We also need two offsets from the start of the area – one for pin on and one for pin off:

```
    uint8_t valoffsetOn = 0x34;
    uint8_t valoffsetOff = 0x4c;
```

We need a mask that is written to the location to change the state of the pin – this also depends on the pin number:

```
    uint32_t mask=(uint32_t)(1 << (pin % 32));
```

Finally we can actually write to the pin:

```
*(volatile uint32_t*) (loc + valoffsetOn) = mask;
```

to set it high and

```
*(volatile uint32_t*) (loc + valoffsetOff) = mask;
```

to set it low.

The complete program with the necessary includes and initialization is:

```
#include <stdio.h>
#include <unistd.h>
#include <sys/mman.h>
#include <sys/stat.h>

uint8_t* load_memmap();

int main()
{
 mraa_init();
 mraa_gpio_context pin31 = mraa_gpio_init(31);
 mraa_gpio_dir(pin31, MRAA_GPIO_OUT);

 load_memmap();
 int pin= 44;

 uint32_t mask=(uint32_t)(1 << (pin % 32));
 uint8_t valoffsetOn = 0x34;
 uint8_t valoffsetOff = 0x4c;

 uint8_t* loc=(pin / 32) * sizeof(uint32_t)+ mmap_reg;

 for (;;) {
  *(volatile uint32_t*) (loc + valoffsetOn) = mask;
  *(volatile uint32_t*) (loc + valoffsetOff) = mask;
 }
 return MRAA_SUCCESS;
}

uint8_t* load_memmap(){
 int mmap_fd;
 struct stat fd_stat;
 uint8_t* mmap_reg;
 mmap_fd = open(
  "/sys/devices/pci0000:00/0000:00:0c.0/resource0",
  O_RDWR);
 fstat(mmap_fd, &fd_stat);
 mmap_reg =(uint8_t*) mmap(NULL, fd_stat.st_size,
   PROT_READ | PROT_WRITE, MAP_FILE | MAP_SHARED,
   mmap_fd, 0);
 return mmap_reg;
}
```

Notice that pin mraa pin 31 is SYSFS pin 44.

All of this isn't very difficult but it is fairly pointless. Most of the pulses produced are about 0.2 microseconds with the occasional pulse around 0.25 microseconds. However at this speed the pulse shape is poor and capacitive effects start to make a difference to the high and low times. If you are using a logic analyzer then the pulse width you measure depends on the thresholds it uses. There seems to be only a small overhead in using the mraa read/write functions. Notice also that as the memory mapping isn't organized into registers you can't make use of it to set or unset multiple pins at a time.

Summary

1. Using standard SYSFS I/O the Edison works with signals in the 20 to 50 microsecond region.

2. Using fast memory mapped I/O you can work with signals in from 0.25 microsecond output with around 5 microsecond inputs.

3. For fast I/O busy wait is the only way to achieve these higher speeds.

4. Fast I/O not only allows you to work with faster pulses it also permits better synchronization between switching multiple I/O lines.

5. You can make use of direct read/writes to the memory mapped drivers and bypass mraa, but the gains are small.

Chapter 6

Near Realtime Linux

You can write realtime programs using standard Linux as long as you know how to control scheduling. In fact it turns out to be relatively easy and it enables the Edison to do things you might not think it capable of.

If you are writing a realtime system there are two things that should concern you – how fast the system can act and how poor this response can be in the worst case.

After learning how to generate accurate and fast pulses, we now have the ability to work with I/O down in the 10 microsecond region, but we still have the problem that our program can be interrupted at any time by the operating system. This means that our outputs and inputs can go drastically wrong. For example, if you generate a fast pulse train in the 10 microsecond range using a standard GPIO line and set a logic analyzer to trigger on a long pulse, you will eventually find one or more very long pulses – typically in the millisecond range. This problem becomes worse the more the CPU is loaded as the operating system switches between tasks to make sure that everything has an opportunity to progress.

The Problem

If you are familiar with microcontrollers such as the PIC, AMTEL or any dedicated MCU then this idea that there could be something getting between you and the hardware will be new. The majority of simple mcus do nothing but run the program you download. Any talk of an "operating system" generally refers to code that does the downloading or minimal system preparation. When you write a control loop then you can safely assume that the loop will run as you wrote it and without interruption - unless of course you have coded an interrupt handler. The point is that in many situations your program is the only program running and you are in complete charge of the processor.

In the case of running a program on the Edison's dual-core Atom the situation is very different. Your program is just one of a number of programs running at any given time. The Edison has two cores and this means that two programs can be running at any given time. The operating system is responsible for starting and stopping programs so that each and every program has a turn.

This is called scheduling and it is a problem if you are trying to write a realtime system.

The problem is that you might write a program that toggles a GPIO line between high and low with a given timing, but whether this timing is honored depends on not just your program but on the operating system as well. You can't even be sure how the operating system will treat your program because it depends in a fairly complex way on what else is running on the system and exactly what the other programs are doing.

Sometimes this is expressed as your program execution being non-deterministic whereas in a simple MCU it is deterministic. This means that if you run the same program twice on on the Edison you probably don't get exactly the same result but on an MCU this is a reasonable expectation.

The whole subject of multitasking operating systems, and scheduling in particular, is a large one and it is usually taught as part of a computer science degree, but generally not as it applies to realtime programming. What this means is that there is often a lot of guesswork involved in getting programs with realtime demands to work properly under general operating systems such as Linux. In fact it is often stated that you can't do realtime processing under Linux because you cannot even place a bound, an upper limit, on how long your program might be suspended by the OS. This isn't true and realtime processing on standard Linux is possible, as long as you are able to live within the constraints.

As an alternative you could opt to run a specially designed realtime OS that does provide guarantees on how quickly a request will be serviced. For example, the Quark MCU in the Edison runs the Viper RTOS. There are also realtime versions of Linux that you can install, but since version 2.6 the Linux Kernel has had sufficient realtime facilities for many applications, so you don't need to move to anything different to the standard Yocto Linux that comes with the Edison.

Before we continue it is important to realize that there is no way that a realtime operating system can increase the speed of operation of the processor. That is, the maximum speed of operation cannot be improved upon. In the case of the Edison this means that you can achieve pulse times if around 10 microseconds if you are careful and no amount of realtime programming is going to improve on this.

What realtime provides is higher consistency of that response time. It isn't perfect, however, and after we have used all of the features of realtime Linux there will still be small periods of time when your program isn't operating and there is little to be done about this.

Realtime Scheduling

Every Linux thread is assigned a scheduling policy and a static priority.

The normal scheduling algorithm, SCHED_OTHER, that Linux uses applies to all threads with static priority zero. If you are not using realtime scheduling then all the threads run at priority zero. In place of a static priority each thread is assigned a dynamic priority, which increases each time it is passed over for execution by the scheduler. The scheduler gives the thread with the highest dynamic priority an opportunity to run for one quantum of time or for one time slice. A thread can be suspended before its time slice is up because it has to wait for I/O or because it is blocked in some other way. Any time a thread makes system call it is also a candidate to be suspended in favor of another thread.

You have only a little control over the computation of the dynamic priority. All you can do is set its initial value using either the nice command or setpriority.

The normal scheduling algorithm doesn't provide much control over what runs. It is "fair" in the sense that all threads get a turn at running, but it isn't possible to set a thread to have a high priority so that it runs in preference to all others. To do this we need to look at the realtime scheduling options.

The most important for us is SCHED_FIFO and sometimes the closely related SCHED_RR. These apply to threads, realtime threads, with static priorities 1 to 99(high).

The first thing to note is that a thread with priority greater than zero will always run in preference to a thread with priority zero and so all realtime threads will run before a thread using the normal scheduling algorithm.

What happens in FIFO is that the system maintains queues of threads that are ready to run at each priority. It then looks for the list with the highest priority with threads ready to run and it starts the thread at the head of the list. When a thread is started it is added to the back of its priority queue. Once a FIFO thread gets to run it can be preempted by a thread with a higher static priority that is ready to run.

If a FIFO thread is suspended because of a higher priority thread it goes back to the head of the queue. This makes it the next thread to resume. This is the sense in which the schedule is First In First Out FIFO; if a thread is suspended by another thread of higher priority that becomes runnable then it is restarted as soon as that thread that replaced it is suspended or stops running.

Finally if a thread explicitly yields (by calling yield) it goes to the end of its priority queue.

Setting Scheduling Priority

This sounds like chaos, but if you think about it for a moment you will see that it provides most of what you are looking for. You are in full control of the Edison and so you can determine exactly how many non-zero priority threads there are. By default all of the standard threads are priority zero and scheduled by the normal scheduler.

Now consider what happens if you start a FIFO scheduled thread with priority 1. It starts and is added to the end of the priority 1 queue. Of course, it is the only priority 1 process and so it starts immediately on one of the two cores available. If the process never makes a call that causes it to wait for I/O say or become blocked in some other way then it will execute without being interrupted by any other process.

In principle this should ensure that your process never delivers anything but its fastest response time. This is almost but not quite true. There are more complex situations you can invent with threads at different priorities according to how important they are but this gets complicated very quickly.

A modification to the SCHED_FIFO scheduler is SCHED_RR – for Round Robin. In this case everything works as for SCHED_FIFO except that each running process is only allowed to run for a single time slice. When the time slice is up, the thread at the head of the priority queue is started and the current thread is added to the end of the queue. You can see that this allows each thread to run for around one time slice in turn as you would expect from a round robin scheduler.

In most cases for realtime programming with the Edison the SCHED_FIFO scheduler is what you need and in its simplest form.

The complete set of scheduling commands are:

- sched_setscheduler Set the scheduling policy and parameters of a specified thread

- sched_getscheduler Return the scheduling policy of a specified thread

- sched_setparam Set the scheduling parameters of a specified thread

- sched_getparam Fetch the scheduling parameters of a specified thread

- sched_get_priority_max Return the maximum priority available in a specified scheduling policy

- sched_get_priority_min Return the minimum priority available in a specified scheduling policy

- sched_rr_get_interval Fetch the quantum used for threads that are scheduled under the "round-robin" scheduling policy

- sched_yield Cause the caller to relinquish the CPU, so that some other thread be executed

- sched_setaffinity Set the CPU affinity of a specified thread
- sched_getaffinity Get the CPU affinity of a specified thread
- sched_setattr Set the scheduling policy and parameters of a specified thread; this Linux-specific system call provides a superset of the functionality of sched_setscheduler and sched_setparam
- sched_getattr Fetch the scheduling policy and parameters of a specified thread; this Linux-specific system call provides a superset of the functionality of sched_getscheduler and sched_getparam.

The scheduling types supported are:

SCHED_OTHER the standard round-robin time-sharing policy

SCHED_BATCH for "batch" style execution of processes

SCHED_IDLE for running very low priority background jobs

SCHED_FIFO a first-in, first-out policy

SCHED_RR a round-robin policy

where only the final two are realtime schedulers.

Also notice that all of the scheduling function return an error code which you should check to make sure thing have worked. For simplicity the examples that follow ignore this advice.

How Bad Is The Problem?

The first question we need to answer is how bad the situation is without realtime scheduling.

This is not an easy question to answer because it depends on so many factors. Take, for example, a very simple program which toggles a GPIO line as fast as it can using mraa:

```
#include <stdio.h>
#include <stdlib.h>
#include "mraa.h"
#include <sched.h>
int main() {
 mraa_gpio_context pin = mraa_gpio_init(13);
 mraa_gpio_dir(pin, MRAA_GPIO_OUT);
 for (;;) {
  mraa_gpio_write(pin, 0);
  mraa_gpio_write(pin, 1);
 }
 return MRAA_SUCCESS;
}
```

As already discovered, we can generate pulses of around 15 microseconds wide using this method. The real question is how does the scheduler change this pulse length by interrupting your program?

Inspecting about one second's worth of readings with a logic analyzer reveals that the pulse length can be as large as 100 microseconds:

Average	14.88
Max	106.88
Min	14.12

A frequency count of pulse sizes is also interesting:

Microseconds	No. of pulses
0	0
10	0
20	65700
30	58
40	0
50	0
60	84
70	12
80	0
90	0
100	0
200	2
10000	0

You can see that there were nearly 100 pulses in the 60-70 microsecond range and just two in the 100-200 range.

This might not seem too bad, but if the CPU is loaded just a little then things look much worse. Add eight CPU-hogging processes and the results are:

Average	15.49
Max	10090.06
Min	14.19

The revised frequencies are:

Microseconds	No. of pulses
0	0
10	0
20	65701
30	56
40	2
50	0
60	35
70	49
80	10
90	0
100	0
20000	4
30000	0
>30000	0

With these conditions there were four instances of greater than 10 millisecond pulses. This means that the program was suspended for 40 milliseconds in a one second sample.

If you try the same thing using fast mraa memory mapping you will find that you get few interruptions on a lightly loaded system as long as you don't make a system call like usleep. If the loading is increased, however, the thread is suspended for increasingly large amounts of time.

Realtime FIFO Scheduling

Now we can try the same test but with FIFO realtime scheduling selected.

To do this we need to use the sched_setscheduler function:

```
sched_setscheduler(pid,SCHED_FIFO,&priority);
```

where pid is the thread id; if it is zero the calling thread is used.

The second parameter sets the type of scheduling used, FIFO in this case, and the final parameter is a pointer to a structure that specifies the priority.

The modified program is:

```
#include <stdio.h>
#include <stdlib.h>
#include "mraa.h"
#include <sched.h>
int main() {
 const struct sched_param priority={1};
 sched_setscheduler(0,SCHED_FIFO,&priority);
 mraa_gpio_context pin = mraa_gpio_init(13);
 mraa_gpio_dir(pin, MRAA_GPIO_OUT);
 mraa_gpio_use_mmaped(pin,1);
 for (;;) {
  mraa_gpio_write(pin, 0);
  mraa_gpio_write(pin, 1);
 }
 return MRAA_SUCCESS;
}
```

If you run this program you will discover that the results are very different, no matter what the load on the CPU.

Average	14.88
Max	67.37
Min	13.56

and the frequency table is:

Microseconds	No. of pulses
0	0
10	0
20	65700
30	57
40	1
50	49
60	46
70	3
80	0
90	0
100	0
1000	0
20000	0

You can see that now the only problem is that we have around 100 pulses around 50 microseconds. Looking at the logic analyzer trace reveals that there is a 50-microsecond pulse about every 10 milliseconds.

Notice that this result is independent of CPU loading, the data above is for a heavily loaded CPU. What happens is that the program is loaded into one of the cores and it stays there as there are no other priority one programs running. All of the priority zero programs are scheduled using the other core to run.

You can also try locking the programs memory to stop the system from paging it if other applications need a lot of memory. In practice this isn't a common occurrence on a device like the Edison but if you do need to do it then all you need is a call to mlock in sys/mman.h and to unlock to unlock it. You can lock the current memory or future memory allocations. In most cases it is sufficient to lock current memory unless you are using dynamic memory allocation:

```
mlockall(MCL_CURRENT);
```

In the case of our test program locking memory make no difference as there is plenty of real memory to go around.

Practical FIFO Scheduling

Adding a simple statement makes your program hog one of the processor cores and removes the long interruptions that occur when other threads are scheduled to run.

You might think at this point that the best thing to do is set a priority of 99 and use FIFO scheduling as soon as your program is loaded. However sharing a single core between all of the other processes on the Edison can have some undesirable effects. If you try this you will discover that every so often – about every ten minutes - the WiFi link will fail. The reason is most likely that the WiFi thread doesn't get to run sufficiently often. There are likely to be other more subtle problems.

To avoid these it is a good idea to only enable FIFO scheduling when it is absolutely needed or to use the yield command at regular intervals.

For example if you are writing a program that has to decode an incoming pulse stream then FIFO scheduling it for the time it actually does the decoding is the best option. In this situation you would still have to cope with a possible 50 microsecond delay every 10 milliseconds.

This raises the question of where the 50 microsecond delay originates?

Without more information it is difficult to be sure, but the most likely suspect is a System Management Interrupt, SMI. This is used by all Intel ICH chip sets including the Atom. An SMI is something that happens outside of the operating system and it is often necessary for the correct operation of the hardware. The bottom line is that SMIs cannot easily be turned off and this problem that effects all operating systems, including realtime operating systems.

At this point things get complicated and you have to start worrying about power management issues, DMA and many other things that a complex CPU and operating system does behind the scenes.

If you can't work within the FIFO restrictions then you are probably better off finding a completely different solution – use an MCU, perhaps even the MCU on the Edison chip, or use dedicated hardware that carries out the operation away from the software like the UART or the PWM GPIO lines. More about this approach in the next chapter.

Summary

1. Linux is not a real-time operating system and provides no guarantees on how long anything takes to receive attention. It does however have some scheduling options that make real-time operation more possible.

2. For threads that interact with hardware you can set FIFO scheduling.

3. In FIFO is that the system maintains queues of threads that are ready to run at each priority. It then looks for the list with the highest priority with threads ready to run and it starts the thread at the head of the list.

4. When a thread is started it is added to the back of its priority queue.

5. Once a FIFO thread gets to run it can be preempted by a thread with a higher static priority that is ready to run.

6. If a FIFO thread is suspended because of a higher priority thread it goes back at the head of the queue. This makes it the next thread to resume. This is the sense in which the schedule is First In First Out FIFO – if a thread is suspended by another thread of higher priority that becomes runnable then it is restarted as soon as that thread that replaced it is suspended or stops running.

7. Finally if a thread explicitly yields (by calling yield) it goes to the end of its priority queue.

8. If you set a single FIFO thread then it is going to run until it yields control to the OS and this is generally all we need to ensure that real-time tasks work properly.

9. Unfortunately even a high priority FIFO thread will still be interrupted by the system but the problem is much less than without the use of FIFO.

Chapter 7

Pulse Width Modulation - PWM

One way around the problem of getting a fast response from a microcontroller is to move the problem away from the processor. In the case of the Edison there are three facilities which can be used to generate signals or communicate with other devices without having to worry about how fast the processor can do the job. In this chapter we take a close look at pulse width modulation including, driving LEDs and servos.

The GPIO lines at their most basic output function can be set high or low by the processor. How fast they can be set high or low depends on the speed of the processor. As we discovered in Chapter 5, the Edison can generate pulses in the region of 0.25 microseconds with memory mapped I/O. This means you can generate a pulse train with a frequency of up to 2MHz.

Using the GPIO line in its Pulse Width Modulation (PWM) mode you can generate pulse trains up to 9.6MHz, i.e. pulses as short as just a little more than 0.1 microseconds. The reason for the increase in speed is that the GPIO controls a pulse generator and once set to generate pulses of a specific type the pulse generator just gets on with it without needing any intervention from the GPIO line or the processor. In fact, the pulse output can continue after your program has ended if you forget to reset it.

Of course, even though the PWM line can generate pulses as short as 0.1 microseconds, it can only change the pulses it produces each time that processor can modify it. For example, you can't use PWM to produce a single 0.1 microsecond pulse because you can't disable the PWM generator in just 0.1 microsecond.

Some Basic Edison PWM Facts

There are some facts worth getting clear right from the start, although some of the meanings will only become clear as we progress.

- It is worth saying – even though it should be fairly obvious – there are no PWM inputs, just 4 outputs. If for some reason you need to decode or respond to a PWM input then you need to program it using the GPIO input lines.

- Unlike the Galileo, which was in many senses the forerunner of the Edison, each of the PWM lines can be set to any period and duty cycle you require – in the case of the Galileo they were all set to the same frequency.

- Although the raw interface with the PWM lines works in nanoseconds, the smallest period you can set is 1 microsecond. You can set a duty cycle smaller than 1 microsecond, however.

- There is no fast memory mapped I/O for the PWM lines as there is for the general GPIO lines. All use of the PWM lines goes through the SYSFS file system and hence is slow – about 10 microseconds for any operation.

- The default period is 50 microseconds. So if you are trying for a specific period but see a 50 microsecond repeat rate, your program is probably not setting the period.

- The fastest pulse repetition rate is 1 microsecond and the slowest is 0.218453 seconds. That is, you can't use a PWM line to flash an LED once every second.

- The PWM lines are not automatically reset when you start a program and this can be a problem, i.e. you inherit whatever the PWM lines were doing when your program starts, more of this later.

- If your PWM using program seems not to work reboot the Edison and try again before you assume there is something seriously wrong.

- As for all of the GPIO lines on the mini-breakout board, the PWM lines work at 1.8V and you need some extra hardware to make them drive anything useful.

- On the Arduino breakout board the PWM lines can be mapped to any of the standard Arduino PWM lines – this isn't necessary or possible on the mini-breakout board.

Mraa PWM commands

There are four PWM GPIO lines:

MRAA Number	Physical Pin	Edison Pin (SYSFS)	Pinmode0	Pinmode1
0	J17-1	GP182	GPIO-182	PWM2
14	J18-1	GP13	GPIO-13	PWM1
20	J18-7	GP12	GPIO-12	PWM0
21	J18-8	GP183	GPIO-183	PWM3

You can use these lines either as standard GPIO lines or as PWM lines and you can switch between modes of operation as you please.

To use one in PWM mode you have to initialize it using one of the init functions;

```
mraa_pwm_init (int pin)
mraa_pwm_init_raw (int chipid, int pin)
```

As usual the first init function uses the mraa pin number and the second uses the GPIO number (SYSFS).

So far so easy – but now the confusion starts. There are lots of ways of setting the output pulse characteristics of the pin. Some might say too many, but as you get used to them you will realize that each one has its particular advantage.

There are two basic things to specify about the pulse train that is generated – its repetition rate and the width of each pulse. The basic way to specify the repetition rate is to use one of the period functions:

```
mraa_pwm_period (mraa_pwm_context dev, float seconds)
mraa_pwm_period_ms (mraa_pwm_context dev, int ms)
mraa_pwm_period_us (mraa_pwm_context dev, int us)
```

It is important to realize that you can't set any time you care to. On the current version of the Edison the PWM lines are constrained to 1 microsecond up to 218453 microseconds, i.e. 0.218453 seconds. If you set a time in any unit outside of this range then the PWM line is not updated.

This can cause you to believe that your program has a bug and the PWM line is not responding.

So for example:

```
mraa_pwm_period_us (pindev, 100);
```

sets the period to 100 microseconds. That is a pulse will be generated every 100 microseconds, but how wide is the pulse?

This is set by one of the pulsewidth functions:

```
mraa_pwm_pulsewidth(mraa_pwm_context dev,float seconds)

mraa_pwm_pulsewidth_ms(mraa_pwm_context dev,int ms)
mraa_pwm_pulsewidth_us(mraa_pwm_context dev,int us)
```

So, for example, after the previous period function call:

```
mraa_pwm_pulsewidth_us(pin, 10);
```

sets the pulse width to 10 microseconds.

The resulting pulse train can be seen on the logic analyzer trace:

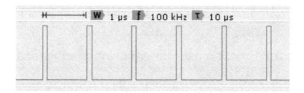

As an alternative to setting the pulse width we can specify percentage of the period that the pulse is high. This is called the duty cycle. For example, a duty cycle of 50% means the pulse is high for half the period and we have a perfect square wave. A duty cycle of 0% is always low and 100% is always high.

To set the duty cycle you can use:

```
mraa_pwm_write (mraa_pwm_context dev, float percentage)
```

where percentage is between 0 and 1 as a fractional percentage.

You can also discover the current duty cycle using:

```
mraa_pwm_read (mraa_pwm_context dev)
```

Often you find that using PWM you set the period once and then modify the duty cycle repeatedly – hence the two sets of functions to set each value.

There are times when setting both period and pulse width/duty cycle is useful and for this we have:

```
mraa_pwm_config_ms(mraa_pwm_context dev,int period,float width)
```

which sets the period in whole milliseconds and the pulse width in milliseconds; and:

```
mraa_pwm_config_percent(mraa_pwm_context dev,int period, float duty)
```

which sets the period in whole milliseconds and duty cycle as a fraction between 0 and 1.

You need also need to know about:

```
mraa_pwm_enable (mraa_pwm_context dev, int enable)
```

which can be used to turn the pulse train on and off. If enable is greater than zero then the pin is driven, otherwise it is disabled.

If you have finished with the pin as a PWM output you can close it using:

```
mraa_pwm_close (mraa_pwm_context dev)
```

and then reuse it as a GPIO pin.

You can also discover the max and min workable periods with:

```
int mraa_pwm_get_max_period()
int mraa_pwm_get_min_period()
```

Using PWM

So now you know how to make use of the PWM lines. All you have to do is initialize one of the four possible pins and set the period and pulse width/duty cycle – as soon as you enable the output the pulse train starts.

The simplest PWM program you can write is:

```
#include "mraa.h"
#include <stdio.h>
#include <unistd.h>
int main()
{
 mraa_pwm_context pwm = mraa_pwm_init(14);
 mraa_pwm_period_us(pwm, 10);
 mraa_pwm_pulsewidth_us(pwm,1);
 mraa_pwm_enable(pwm,1 );

 return MRAA_SUCCESS;
}
```

This produces a pulse train consisting of a microsecond wide pulse every then microseconds on mraa pin 14 which is J18-1 on the mini-breakout board.

Notice that there is no need to put the program into an infinite loop. Once the PWM line has been set up and enables it just gets on with generating the pulse train no matter what the Edison does. In this case the pulse generation continues long after the program has ended.

Just to demonstrate that all of the PWM lines can be used independently of one another here is a program that sets each one of the four to a different period and duty cycle:

```
#include "mraa.h"
#include <stdio.h>
#include <unistd.h>int main()
{
 mraa_pwm_context pwm0 = mraa_pwm_init(20);
 mraa_pwm_context pwm1 = mraa_pwm_init(14);
 mraa_pwm_context pwm2 = mraa_pwm_init(0);
 mraa_pwm_context pwm3 = mraa_pwm_init(21);
 mraa_pwm_period_us(pwm0, 10);
 mraa_pwm_period_us(pwm1, 20);
 mraa_pwm_period_us(pwm2, 30);
 mraa_pwm_period_us(pwm3, 40);
 mraa_pwm_write(pwm0, 0.5f);
 mraa_pwm_write(pwm1, 0.4f);
 mraa_pwm_write(pwm2, 0.3f);
 mraa_pwm_write(pwm3, 0.2f);
 mraa_pwm_enable(pwm0,1 );
 mraa_pwm_enable(pwm1,1 );
 mraa_pwm_enable(pwm2,1 );
 mraa_pwm_enable(pwm3,1 );
```

```
 return MRAA_SUCCESS;
}
```

You can see the result in the following logic analyzer display:

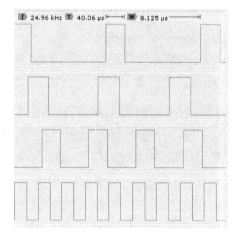

If you want to make sure that you don't inherit any settings from a previous program and want to make sure that your settings do update any existing ones it is a good idea to disable the PWM lines before you use them.

That is:

```
mraa_pwm_context pwm0 = mraa_pwm_init(20);
mraa_pwm_context pwm1 = mraa_pwm_init(14);
mraa_pwm_context pwm2 = mraa_pwm_init(0);
mraa_pwm_context pwm3 = mraa_pwm_init(21);
mraa_pwm_enable(pwm0,0 );
mraa_pwm_enable(pwm1,0 );
mraa_pwm_enable(pwm2,0 );
mraa_pwm_enable(pwm3,0 );
```

How Fast?

Of course in most cases the whole point is to vary the duty cycle or the period of the pulse train for reasons that will be discussed later. Occasionally the issue of how fast a pulse can be created arises and this is a surprisingly difficult question to answer.

If you use the max and min period functions to print the values to the Eclipse console with something like:

```
printf("min %d \n", mraa_pwm_get_min_period ());
printf("max %d \n", mraa_pwm_get_max_period ());
```

you will see

```
min 1
max 218453
```

or 1 to around 0.22 seconds, which corresponds to a max frequency of 1MHz and a minimum frequency of around 4.6Hz.

The next question is how fast can you change the characteristic of a PWM line? In other words, how fast can you change the duty cycle? There is no easy way to give an exact answer but if you change the duty cycle in a tight loop you will discover that a period of 12 microseconds gives a train with one pulse of each type:

```
mraa_pwm_context pwm0 = mraa_pwm_init(20);
mraa_pwm_enable(pwm0,0 );
mraa_pwm_period_us(pwm0, 12);
mraa_pwm_enable(pwm0,1 );
for (;;) {
 mraa_pwm_write(pwm0, 0.5f);
 mraa_pwm_write(pwm0, 0.25f);
}
return MRAA_SUCCESS;
}
```

What this means is that the pulse duty cycle is being changed at the same rate as the pulses are generated. Increasing or decreasing the period slightly, the result is a slow phase shift. You can therefore infer that the time to update is about 12 microseconds, which is in line with the shortest pulse times on the SYSFS driven GPIO lines.

As in the case of the GPIO lines, you can't expect to make changes to more than one line in 12 microseconds. Each change that you make takes around that time. For PWM lines in many uses this isn't a problem because the pulse time is typically milliseconds and 12 microseconds is more than fast enough. However there are PWM applications, for example pulse width coding, where it could be a real problem.

Uses of PWM – Driving LEDs

What sorts of things do you use PWM for?

There are lots of very clever uses for PWM. For example, you can already use it to create pulse trains that would be difficult to create in any other way – a one microsecond pulse train for example. However there are two use cases which account for most PWM applications - power modulation and signaling to servos.

The first, power modulation, is expressed more simply as "dimming an LED". By changing the duty cycle of the PWM pulse train you can set the amount of power delivered to an LED, or any other device, and hence change its brightness. The amount of power delivered to a device by a pulse train is proportional to the duty cycle. A pulse train that has a 50% duty cycle is delivering current to the load only 50% of the time and this is irrespective of the pulse repetition rate. So duty cycle controls the power, but the period still matters in many situations because you want to avoid any flashing or other effects. A higher frequency smooths out the power flow at any duty cycle.

You can use a PWM supply to control the brightness of an LED for example, or the rotation rate of a DC motor. The only differences in applications such as these are to do with the voltage and current you need to control and the way duty cycle relates to whatever the physical effect is. For example, for an LED we might use a 5V supply and a current of a few tens of milliamps. In the case of an LED the connection between duty cycle and brightness is a complicated matter, but the simplest approach uses the fact that the perceived brightness is roughly proportional to the cube root of the input power. The exact relationship is more complicated, but this is good enough for most applications. As the power supplied to the LED is proportional to the duty cycle we have:

$$d = k\, b^3$$

where b is the perceived brightness and d is the duty cycle. Notice that as the LED is either full on or full off there is no effect of the change in LED light output with current – the LED is always run at the same current.

What all of this means is that if you want an LED to fade in a linear fashion you need to change the duty cycle in a non-linear fashion. Intuitively it means that changes when the duty cycle is small produce bigger changes in brightness than when the duty cycle is large. For a simple example we need to connect a standard LED to the PWM line.

Given that all of the Edison's lines work at 1.8V and most LEDs need more voltage than this, we also need a transistor to drive the LED. You could use a FET (Field Effect Transistor), but for this sort of application an old-fashioned Bipolar Junction Transistor (BJT) works very well, is cheap and available in a through-hole mount, i.e. it comes with wires. Almost any general purpose npn BJT transistor will work, but the 2N2222 is a very common option.

You can use pin j20-1 to supply the 5V and pin J19-3 is ground. The PMW0 line is J18-7. If you are using the 2N222 the pinouts are:

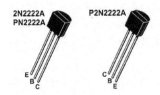

As always the positive terminal on the LED is the long pin.

Assuming that you have this circuit constructed then a simple PWM program to modify its brightness from low to high and back to low in a loop is;

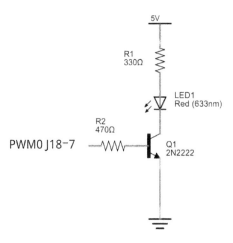

```
#include "mraa.h"
#include <stdio.h>
#include <unistd.h>
int main()
{
 mraa_pwm_context pwm0 = mraa_pwm_init(20);
 mraa_pwm_enable(pwm0,0 );
 mraa_pwm_period_ms(pwm0,1);
 mraa_pwm_enable(pwm0,1 );
 int w=1;
 int inc=1;
 for (;;) {
  mraa_pwm_pulsewidth_us (pwm0, w);
  w=w+inc;
  if(w>100 || w<2)inc=(-1)*inc;
  usleep(1000);
 }
 return MRAA_SUCCESS;
}
```

The basic idea is to set up a pulse train with a period of 1ms. Next, in the for loop, the duty cycle is set to 1 to 100 microseconds and then 100 back down to 1 microsecond. Although this is just a duty cycle of around 0 to 10%, it provides a good range of brightness. You can experiment with the limits for your LED. Notice that the way that the loop counts up and down is to use inc, which is either 1 or -1 and using the age old trick of flipping between 1 and -1 and back again by multiplying by -1.

Changing the LED Brightness

What about a linear change in brightness?

To achieve this reasonably accurately isn't difficult. All we need to do is increase the power, or equivalently the duty cycle, in steps that are cubic. If we just use 0 to 10 cubed we get a pulse width of 0 to 1000, which is ideal for our 1ms pulse used in the previous example, i.e. 0 to 100% duty cycle.

If we were working with a simple microcontroller then at this point we would need to consider using a lookup table for the steps as a way of increasing the performance. The Edison however has plenty of number crunching power so a direct implementation is possible:

```
#include "mraa.h"
#include <stdio.h>
#include <unistd.h>
int main()
{
 mraa_pwm_context pwm0 = mraa_pwm_init(20);
 mraa_pwm_enable(pwm0,0 );
 mraa_pwm_period_ms(pwm0,1);
 mraa_pwm_enable(pwm0,1 );

 int w=0;
 int b=0;
 int inc=1;
 for (;;) {
  b+=inc;
  w=b*b*b;
  mraa_pwm_pulsewidth_us (pwm0, w);
  if(w>=1000 || w<=0)inc=(-1)*inc;
  usleep(40000);
 }
 return MRAA_SUCCESS;
}
```

As this produces 10 cubic steps,, a usleep of 40,000 makes each step last 4ms and so it takes 40ms to go from low to high.

If you replace the delay with a value of 100,000 then you will get a 1 second cycle which, using only ten steps, starts to look a little unsteady. You can increase the number of steps by simply dividing by a suitable factor. Dividing by 10 produces roughly 20 cubic step to get to 1000.

At this point you would probably decide that a lookup table is essential, but again the Edison has no problem doing floating point arithmetic for this sort of problem:

```
float w=0;
float b=0;
float inc=1;
for (;;) {
 b+=inc;
 w=b*b*b/10;
 mraa_pwm_pulsewidth_us (pwm0,(int) w);
 if(w>=1000 || w<=0)inc=(-1)*inc;
 usleep(50000);
}
```

Notice that now as there are twice as many steps we only need each one to last half the time, i.e. 50,000 microseconds.

In most cases exactly how linear the response of the LED is is irrelevant. The only exception is when you are trying to drive LEDs to create a grey level or color display.

Controlling a Servo

Hobby servos, the sort used in radio control models, are very cheap and easy to use and the Edison has enough PWM lines to control four of them without much in the way of extras.

A basic servo has just three connections, usually ground and power line and a signal line. The colors used vary, but usually the power is red, the ground line black or brown and the signal line white, yellow or orange. The power wire has to be connected to 5V supply capable of providing enough current to run the motor, anything up to 500mA or more depending on the servo.

The good news is that the servo signal line generally needs very little current, although it does need to be switched between 0 and 5V using a PWM signal.

You can assume that the signal line needs to be driven as a voltage load and so the appropriate way to drive the servo is:

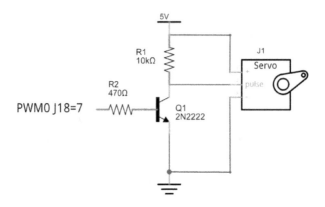

The resistor R1 can be a lot larger than 10K for most servos – 47K often works.

Now all we have to do is set the PWM line to produce 20ms pulses with pulse widths ranging from 1 to 2 ms. If you implement this as a simple program you will discover that the servo does nothing at all – apart perhaps from vibrating. The reason is that the transistor voltage driver is an inverter. When the PWM line is high the transistor is fully on and the servo's pulse line is effectively grounded. When the PWM line is low the transistor is fully off and the servo's pulse line is pulled high by the resistor.

A common solution to this problem is to drive the servo using an emitter follower configuration, but in this case this isn't possible because the maximum voltage such a configuration would generate is 1.8-0.6=1.2V, which is too low to drive most servos. The standard solution in this case is to use two transistors to generate a non-inverted pulse, but it is possible to use a single transistor in a non-inverting configuration as explained in Chapter 11.

The simplest solution of all is to ignore the problem in hardware and solve the problem in software. After all, this is the main advantage of using a processor rather than custom electronics. Instead of generating 20ms pulses with pulse widths 1 to 2ms, you can generate an inverted pulse with 20ms pulses with widths in the range 18 to 19 ms.

The following program moves the servo between its two extreme positions and back again:

```c
#include "mraa.h"
#include <stdio.h>
#include <unistd.h>

int main()
{
 mraa_pwm_context pwm3 = mraa_pwm_init(21);
 mraa_pwm_enable(pwm3,0 );
 mraa_pwm_period_ms(pwm3,20);
 mraa_pwm_enable(pwm3,1 );
 for (;;) {
  mraa_pwm_pulsewidth_us (pwm3,20000-1000);
  sleep(4);
  mraa_pwm_pulsewidth_us (pwm3,20000-1500);
  sleep(4);
  mraa_pwm_pulsewidth_us (pwm3,20000-2000);
  sleep(4);
 }
 return MRAA_SUCCESS;
}
```

If you run this program you should find that the servo moves as promised. However, it might not reach its limits of movement. Servos differ in how they respond to the input signal and you might need to calibrate the pulse widths. Many robot implementations, for example, calibrate the servos to find their maximum movement using either mechanical switches to detect when the servo is at the end of its range or a vision sensor.

You can see from the logic analyzer plot that the PWM pulse train is "inverted" as desired.

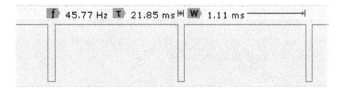

You can also see that the values used for the period and for the pulse width could do with some adjustment to bring them closer to the target values. In practice, however, servo calibration is the better answer.

Given that the Edison has four PWM lines you can drive four servos without any additional hardware. Beyond four servos and you most likely need to use one of the many servo boards that are available. For example, SparkFun has an eight-line PWM board that is driven by the Edison's I2C bus, which is the subject of the next chapter._

What Else Can You Use PWM For?

PWM lines are incredibly versatile and it is always worth asking the question "Could I use PWM?" when you are considering almost any problem. The LED example shows how you can use PWM as a power controller.

You can extend this idea to a computer controlled switch mode power supply. All you need is a capacitor to smooth out the voltage and perhaps a transformer to change the voltage. The same idea can be used as a crude DtoA converter.

Change the LED for an 8-ohm loudspeaker and you have a way of generating sound. At its simplest you can feed the PWM signal into the speaker unmodified and create "space" sounds. However, you can also add a filter and work at a higher pulse rate to create higher quality audio, and all without a USB dongle in sight. You can also use PWM to control the speed of a DC motor and if you add a simple bridge circuit you can control its direction and speed.

Finally, you can use a PWM signal as a modulated carrier for data communications. For example, most infra-red controller make use of a 38KHz carrier, which is roughly a 26 microseconds. This is switched on and off for 1ms and this is well within the range that the Edison PWM can manage. So all you have to do is replace the red LED in the previous circuit with an infra-red LED and you have the start of a remote control or data transmission link.

Summary

1. You can set the pulse repetition rate and duty cycle of the four PWM outputs independently of one another.

2. There are no PWM inputs

3. You can change the duty cycle every 12 microseconds

4. PWM is used to control servos, the brightness of LEDs and generally create a crude DtoA convertor.

Chapter 8

Getting Started with the I2C Bus

The I2C bus is one of the most useful ways of connecting moderately sophisticated sensors and peripherals to the Edison. The only problem is that it can seem like a nightmare confusion of hardware, low level interaction and high level software. There are few general introductions to the subject because at first sight every I2C device is different, but here we present one.

The I2C bus is a serial bus that can be used to connect multiple devices to a controller. It is a simple bus that uses two active wires; one for data and one for a clock. Despite there being lots of problems in using the I2C bus because it isn't well standardized and devices can conflict and generally do things in their own way, it is still commonly used and too useful to ignore.

The big problem in getting started with the I2C bus is that you will find it described at many different levels of detail, such as physical bus characteristics, the protocol, and details of individual devices. It can be difficult to relate all of this together and produce a working anything. In fact you only need to know the general workings of the I2C bus, some general features of the protocol and know the addresses and commands used by any particular device.

To explain and illustrate these idea we really do have to work with a particular device to make things concrete. However the basic stages of getting things to work, the steps, the testing and verification, are more or less the same irrespective of the device.

I2C Hardware Basics

The I2C bus is very simple from the hardware point of view. It has just two signal lines, SDA and SCL, the data and clock lines respectively. Each of these lines is pulled up by a suitable resistor to the supply line at whatever voltage the devices are working at – 3.3V and 5V are common choices but it could be 1.8V as well. The size of the pullup resistors isn't critical, but 4.7K is typical as shown in the circuit diagram

You simply connect the SDA and SCL pins of each of the devices to the pullup resistors. Of course, if any of the devices have built-in pullup resistors you can omit the external resistors. More of a problem is if multiple devices each have pull ups. In this case you need to disable all but one set.

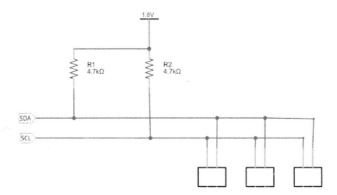

The I2C bus is an open collector bus. This means that it is actively pulled down by a transistor set to on. When the transistor is off, however, the bus returns to the high voltage state via the pullup resistor. The advantage of this approach is that multiple devices can pull the bus low at the same time. That is, an open collector bus is low when one or more devices pulls it low and high when none of the devices is active.

The SCL line provides a clock which is used to set the speed of data transfer – one data bit is presented on the SDA line for each pulse on the SCL line. In most cases the I2C bus has a single master device – the Edison in our case - which drives the clock and invites the slaves to receive or transmit data. Multiple masters are possible, but this is advanced and not often necessary. The Edison cannot work with multiple masters.

At this point we could go into the details of how all of this works in terms of bits. However, the Edison and the mraa software handles these details for us. All you really need to know is that all communication occurs in 8-bit packets. The master sends a packet, an address frame, which contains the address of the slave it wants to interact with. Every slave has to have a unique address – usually 7 bits, but it can be 11 bits and the Edison does support this.

One of the problems in using the I2C bus is that manufacturers often use the same address or same set of selectable addresses and this can make using particular combinations of devices on the same bus difficult or impossible.

The 7-bit address is set as the high order 7 bits in the byte and this can be confusing as an address that is stated as 0x40 in the data sheet results in 0x80 being sent to the device. After sending an address frame the master then sends or receives data frames back from the slave. There are also special signals used to mark the start and end of an exchange of packets but the Edison takes care of these.

This is really all you need to know about I2C in general to get started, but it is worth finding out more of the details as you need them. You almost certainly will need them as you debug I2C programs.

Edison I2C

The Edison supports two I2C buses but only one is usable on the Arduino breakout board and the second often behaves oddly for reasons of lack of support. For this reason it is better to use I2C-1 unless you have a very good reason not to.

The pins used on the mini-breakout board, including ground and power lines that are concerned with I2C:

Mraa Number	Physical Pin	Edison Pin (SYSFS)	Pinmode0	Pinmode1
6	J17-7	GP27	GPIO-27	I2C-6-SCL
7	J17-8	GP20	GPIO-20	I2C-1-SDA
8	J17-9	GP28	GPIO-28	I2C-6-SDA
19	J18-6	GP19	GPIO-19	I2C-1-SCL
29	J19-2	V_V1P80		
30	J19-3	GND		
42	J20-1	V_VSYS		
43	J20-2	V_V3P30		

As we are going to use a 1.8V sensor and I2C bus 1 the pins that we are going to use are:

Physical Pin	
J17-8	I2C 1 SDA
J18-6	I2C-1-SCL
J19-2	V_V1P80
J19-3	GND

The I2C Mraa Functions

The I2C mraa functions are confusing for the usual reason that there are a lot of different options. Let's look at them in groups that do something similar and in the order you would generally use them.

Initialization

The first thing you have to do is initialize the bus you are going to use.

There are two init functions:

- `mraa_i2c_context i2c=mraa_i2c_init(int bus)`

- `mraa_i2c_context i2c=mraa_i2c_init_raw(unsigned int bus)`

For the Edison mini-breakout board you can use bus 1 or 6 in either function.

For example:

```
mraa_i2c_context i2c=mraa_i2c_init(1);
```

will initialize bus 1 and return a context in i2c. If the bus cannot be initialized then the context is NULL.

Initializing the bus has to be done at the start of any use of the I2C bus, but once you have a context you can use it without having to reinitialize the bus. When you have finished using the bus you can call the function:

```
mraa_i2c_stop(mraa_i2c_context dev)
```

Each device on the I2C bus has to have a unique 7-bit address. After initializing the bus and before you send any data you have to set the address of the device you want to interact with:

```
mraa_result_t mraa_i2c_address(i2c, uint8_t address)
```

You can look up the address that each device responds to in its datasheet. Don't worry about any of the low-level descriptions of the way the least significant bit is used to determine if a read or a write is in operation - this is often reported in datasheets as one address for write and one for read. You also need to keep in mind that the 7-bit address is sent as the high order bits in the byte.

For example, a device might report an address of 0x40 on its data sheet. On the bus this would translate to a write address of 0x80 for write and a read address of 0x81, i.e. to write device 0x40 you send 0x80 and to write to it you send 0x81.

For mraa set the 7-bit address and the functions will take care of what code to actually put on the bus, i.e. use 0x40 and mraa will make the necessary changes. Also notice that neither the init or the address function actually causes anything to happen on the I2C bus. They simply set parameters which are used in the subsequent function calls. If you are looking at the I2C bus with a logic analyzer you won't see anything happen when you use init or address.

Write

There are four write functions:

- `mraa_i2c_write_byte(i2c, const uint8_t data)`
- `mraa_i2c_write(i2c, const uint8_t *data, int length)`
- `mraa_i2c_write_byte_data(i2c,`
  `const uint8_t data,const uint8_t command)`
- `mraa_i2c_write_word_data(i2c,`
  `const uint16_t data,const uint8_t command)`

By far the simplest of these is the first one, which writes a single byte of data to the device. How this byte is used by the device generally depends on many things, but it is important to realize that this function actually sends two bytes to the device – an address frame and a data frame. The address frame is a byte containing the address of the device you set earlier and the data byte is the one you have just specified in the function call.

Notice that mraa takes care of all of the details of the protocol. If you know about the I2C protocol then it is worth saying that mraa deals with the start sequence, the address frame with the write bit set to zero; it checks the NAK/ACK bit from the slave, sends the data bit, checks the NAK/ACK bit from the slave and sends the stop sequence.

If you want to send more than a single byte then you need to use one of the other write functions.

- `mraa_i2c_write(i2c, const uint8_t *data, int length)`

will write multiple bytes in exactly the same way as the write_byte function. That is, if you set up a buffer with three bytes:

```
uint8_t buf[3];
//store data in buf
mraa_i2c_write (i2c,buf,3);
```

this will first send an address frame as in the case of write_byte and then follow it up with three data frames containing the data in the buffer.

Notice that this is different to sending three bytes using write_byte three times. The write function only sends one address frame and then multiple data frames. Each time you use the write_byte function an address frame is send and a single data frame. Which one of these functions you use depends on whether the device wants a single byte at a time or a set of bytes.

The final two write functions implement a standard interaction between master and slave - writing data to a register. Many devices have internal storage, indeed some I2C devices are nothing but internal storage, e.g. I2C EPROMs.

In this case a standard transaction is:

1. send address frame
2. send a data frame with the command to select the register
3. send a data frame containing the byte or word to be written to the register

The write_byte_data command writes to a byte register and the write_word_data command writes a word (2 bytes) to a 16-bit register:

- ```
  mraa_i2c_write_byte_data (i2c, const uint8_t data,
                                 const uint8_t command)
  ```

- ```
  mraa_i2c_write_word_data (i2c, const uint16_t data,
                                 const uint8_t command)
  ```

Notice the command that has to be sent depends on the device and you have to look it up in its datasheet. It is also worth knowing that:

```
mraa_i2c_write_byte_data (i2c, data, command)
```

is equivalent to:

```
uint8_t buf[2];
buf[0]=command;
buf[1]=data;
mraa_i2c_write (i2c,buf,2);
```

Next we have to look at how to read data from the device. Notice that in many transactions a read has to be preceded by a write that tells the device what data you want.

Read

There are five read functions which broadly copy what the write functions do:

- ```
  int mraa_i2c_read (i2c, uint8_t *data, int length)
  ```

- ```
  uint8_t mraa_i2c_read_byte (ic2)
  ```

- ```
  uint8_t mraa_i2c_read_byte_data (i2c, const uint8_t command)
  ```

- ```
  uint16_t  mraa_i2c_read_word_data (i2c,const uint8_t command)
  ```

- ```
  int mraa_i2c_read_bytes_data (i2c, uint8_t command,
                                 uint8_t *data, int length)
  ```

As in the case of read the simplest write function is:

- ```
  uint8_t mraa_i2c_read_byte (ic2)
  ```

This sends an address frame and then reads a single byte from the slave. As with the write function, mraa takes care of all of the protocol necessary to send and receive the packets. You also have to use the "write" address of the device the function automatically sets the low order read bit for you.

If you want to read multiple bytes then you can use the function:

- `int mraa_i2c_read (i2c, uint8_t *data, int length)`

You simply have to supply a buffer of the correct length and specify the number of bytes to be read.

There are also three functions for reading data from a register:

- `uint8_t mraa_i2c_read_byte_data (i2c, const uint8_t command)`

- `uint16_t mraa_i2c_read_word_data (i2c, const uint8_t command)`

- `int mraa_i2c_read_bytes_data (i2c, uint8_t command, uint8_t *data, int length)`

This works as per the register read functions where you specify the register as the command parameter.

When reading data you can read a byte and a word register and in addition a register of any size using read_bytes_data. In this case you supply a buffer and a number of bytes to read.

Slow Read

This raises for the first time the question of how we cope with the speed that a slave can or cannot respond to a request for data. There are two broad approaches to waiting for data on the I2C bus.

The first is simply to request the data and then perform reads in a polling loop. If the device isn't ready with the data then it sends a data frame with a NAK bit set. The mraa read functions return a zero if it fails or the data if it doesn't. Of course the polling loop doesn't have to be "tight". The response time is often long enough to do other things and you can use the I2C bus to work with other slave devices while the one you activated gets on with trying to get you the data you requested. All you have to do is to remember to read its data at some later time.

The second way is to allow the slave to hold the clock line low after the master has released it. In most cases the master will simply wait before moving on to the next frame while the clock line is held low. The Edison I2C bus implements this clock stretching protocol and it will wait until the slave releases the clock line before proceeding. This is very simple and it means you don't have to implement a polling loop, but also notice that your program is frozen until the slave releases the clock line.

Many devices implement both types of slow read protocol and you can use whichever suits your application.

There is also the small matter of the speed of the I2C clock. In principle the clock can run at almost any speed, but in practice this usually isn't the case. Most slave devices don't have strict clock rates that have to be used with them as they are designed as static devices synced to whatever SCL clock rate the master cares to use. If it turns out to be too fast then most will use clock stretching. In extreme cases it may be necessary to slow down or even speed up the master's clock.

There is an mraa function to do this:

```
mraa_i2c_frequency (i2c,mode)
```

This works with the Edison if you are using the latest mraa library. You can set one of three modes:

- MRAA_I2C_STD Standard mode 100Kb/s
- MRAA_I2C_FAST Fast mode 400Kb/s
- MRAA_I2C_HIGH High-speed mode 3.4Mb/s

By default the Edison works in Fast mode. You can select Standard mode but at the time of writing the High-speed mode doesn't seem to work.

SYSFS Linux I2C Commands

As with most Linux hardware, the necessary drivers represent the hardware as files. This is how it is with I2C and a collection of I2C tools that you can use from the command line are available. Sometimes these are useful, but in the case of the Edison they tend not to work as well as you might hope – and particularly so with I2C 6.

My advice is not to rely on the information you get back from the Linux tools because they often fail to detect devices that actually exist on the bus.

The commands available are:

To scan the bus report devices connected:

```
i2cdetect
```

To dump registers:

```
i2cdump
```

To read a device register:

```
i2cget
```

To set a device register:

```
i2cset
```

For example, to scan the buses installed you can use:

```
i2cdetect -l
```

This will list eight possible I2C buses on the Edison. Of course, for hardware reasons ,you can only use 2, I2C-1 and I2C-6.

To list all of the devices connected to a bus you can use:

```
i2cdetect -r 1
```

This scans bus 1 and often results in a crash.

To dump all the registers in a particular device on I2C-1 use:

```
i2cdump 1 address w
```

To read a particular register on a particular device use:

```
i2cget 1 address register w
```

Finally to set a particular register on a particular device use:

```
i2cset 1 address register data w
```

Some programmers like using these commands to check that slave devices are present and working. Personally I would prefer to write a C program, simply because the results are more reliable.

If you want to know more about the Linux i2c tools consult the man pages.

Summary

1. The I2C bus is very simple with just two signal lines, SDA and SCL, the data and clock lines respectively.

2. The Edison supports two I2C buses but only one is usable on the Arduino breakout board. For this reason it is better to use I2C-1 unless you have a very good reason not to.

3. Each device on the I2C bus has to have a unique 7-bit address. To set the address of the device you want to interact with use:
   ```
   mraa_i2c_address
   ```

4. Each I2C data packet starts with a device address followed by a number of data bytes. There are mraa functions to send one or multiple bytes.

5. A standard I2C interaction is to read/write data to a register by sending an address frame, sending a data frame with the command to select the register and sending or reading a data frame containing the byte or word to be written to the register.

6. Mraa has functions to read and write data to a register.

7. There are two ways to handle a slow slave device: the master can poll until the data is read in; or the master can allow the slave to hold the clock line until it the data is ready to read. You can use either method with the Edison I2C

8. There are a range of SYSFS commands that you can use to work with I2C at the command line, but these often don't work as expected.

Chapter 9

I2C Measuring Temperature

Using I2C devices is fairly easy once you have successfully used one – and hence know what information you need and what to look for in a working system. In this chapter we use the HTU21D temperature and humidity sensor as a case study of I2C in action. It also happens to be a useful sensor.

Using an I2C device has two problems – the physical connection between master and slave and figuring out what the software has to do to make it work. In this chapter we take the principle outlined in the previous one and add the information in the HTU21D data sheet to make a working temperature humidity sensor using mraa. There is a C++ implementation of the HTU21D in the upm library and you can use this if it is more appropriate to your project. In this case it is the details of the implementation that is important, starting with the hardware.

The SparkFun HTU21D

The HTU21D Humidity and Temperature sensor is one of the easiest of I2C devices to use with the Edison mini-breakout board. The reason is that it works at 1.5V and therefore works with the Edison's 1.8V logic and use its power supply. This means you don't have to worry about level shifting, which simplifies your first encounter with I2C, and it provides an attractive way to measure temperature and humidity in a very small package.

The only problem is that the HTU21D is only available in a surface mount package. To overcome this you could simply solder some wires onto the pads buy a general breakout board. However, it is much simpler to buy the SparkFun HTU21D breakout board because this has easy connections and built-in pull up resistors. This means that you don't need to add any components to get this circuit working – just four connections.

Don't worry about the fact that board and the documentation suggests that this only works at 3.3V – it works "best" at 3.3V, but it also works at 1.8V. If you use the HTU21D breakout then for prototyping the only thing you have to do is solder some pins or wires to the pads.

If you decide to work with some other I2C device you can still follow the steps in this account, but you would have to modify what you do to be correct for the device you are using. In particular if you select a device that works at 3.3V or 5V you need a level converter and you might also need pull-up resistors.

Wiring the HTU21D

As we are going to use a 1.8V sensor and I2C bus 1 the pins that we are going to use are the same as in the previous chapter:

Physical Pin	
J17-8	I2C-1-SDA
J18-6	I2C-1-SCL
J19-2	V_V1P80
J19-3	GND

Given that the HTU21D has pull up resistors and works at 1.8V connecting it to I2C 1 on the Edison is trivial:

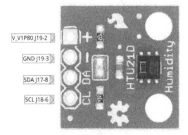

You can use a prototype board to make the connections and this makes it easier to connect other instruments such as a logic analyzer.

A First Program

After wiring up any i2C device the first question that needs to be answered is, "does it work?" Unfortunately for most complex devices finding out if it works is a multi-step process. Our first program will aim to read some data back from the HTU21D, any data will do.

If you look at the data sheet you will find that the device address is 0x40 and its supports the following commands:

Command	Code	Comment
Trigger Temperature Measurement	0xE3	Hold master
Trigger Humidity Measurement	0xE5	Hold master
Trigger Temperature Measurement	0xF3	No Hold master
Trigger Humidity Measurement	0xF5	No Hold master
Write user register	0xE6	
Read user register	0xE7	
Soft Reset	0xFE	

The easiest of these to get started with is the Read user register command. The user register gives the current setup of the device and can be used to set the resolution of the measurement.

Notice that the codes that you send to the device can often be considered addresses or commands. In this case you can think of sending 0xE7 as a command to read the register or the read address of the register – it makes no difference. In most cases the term command is used when sending the code makes the device do something and the term address is used when it simply makes the device read or write specific data.

To read the user register we have to write a byte containing 0xE7 and then read the byte the device sends back. Notice that means sending an address frame, a data frame and then another address frame and reading a data frame.

You can do this in two ways. The first is to use raw byte read and write commands:

```
mraa_i2c_context i2c;
i2c = mraa_i2c_init(1);
mraa_i2c_address(i2c, 0x40);
mraa_i2c_write_byte(i2c,0xE7);
uint8_t data = mraa_i2c_read_byte(i2c);
printf("Register= %d \n", data);
```

This program sets up I2C-1, sets the address to 0x40 and then sends 0xE7 and immediately reads a byte that the device sends back.

If you run this program you will see:

```
Register= 66
```

this is the default value of the register and it corresponds to a resolution of 12 and 14 bits for the humidity and temperature respectively.

In Detail

If you have a logic analyzer that can interpret the I2C protocol connected, what you will see is:

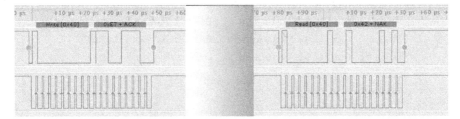

You can see that the write_byte function sends an address packet set to the device's 7-bit address 0x40 as the high order bits and the low order bit set to zero to indicate a write. After this you get a data packet containing 0xE7. After a few milliseconds it sends the address frame again, only this time with the low order bit set to 1 to indicate a read and it then receives back a single byte of data from the device – the 0x42 corresponding to the 66 decimal reported.

As this is a standard send a command/register address and receive back a single byte we can perform exactly the same task using the read_byte_data function which does the write and the read as a single operation:

```
mraa_i2c_context i2c;
i2c = mraa_i2c_init(1);
mraa_i2c_address(i2c, 0x40);
uint8_t data =mraa_i2c_read_byte_data (i2c, 0xE7);
printf("Register= %d \n", data);
```

If you run this program you will get the same result. However if you look at the logic analyzer result you will see:

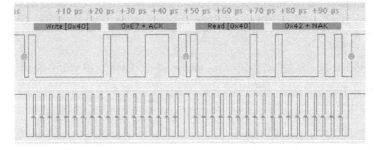

The same address and data frames are sent and received but now there is no delay between the first two and the last two. This is the advantage of using the command-oriented mraa functions.

Reading the Raw Temperature Data

Now we come to reading one of the two quantities that the device measures, temperature. If you look back at the command table you will see that there are two possible commands for reading the temperature:

Command	Code	Comment
Trigger Temperature Measurement	0xE3	Hold master
Trigger Temperature Measurement	0xF3	No Hold master

What is the difference between Hold master and No Hold master?

This was discussed in the previous chapter in a general setting. The device cannot read the temperature instantaneously and the master can either opt to be held waiting for the data, i.e. hold master, or released to do something else and poll for the data until it is ready.

The hold master option works by allowing the device to stretch the clock pulse by holding the line low after the master has released it. In this mode the master will wait until the device releases the line. Not all masters support this mode, but the Edison does making this the simpler option. To read the temperature using the Hold master mode you simply send 0xE3 and then read three bytes.

As with the simple read register command there are two ways of doing this. You can use the write_byte function to send the command and then use the read function to read three bytes. Notice you cannot use the read_byte function three times to read the bytes the device sends because this would send three address frames, rather than the one required. The program is:

```
uint8_t buf[3];
mraa_i2c_write_byte(i2c,0xE3);
mraa_i2c_read(i2c, buf, 3);
uint8_t msb= buf[0];
uint8_t lsb= buf[1];
uint8_t check= buf[2];
printf("msb %d \n lsb %d \n checksum %d \n", msb,lsb,check);
```

The buffer is unpacked into three variables with more meaningful names: msb – most significant byte, lsb – least significant byte, and check(sum).

If the temperature is in the 20C range, you should see something like:

```
msb 97
lsb 232
checksum 217
```

The logic analyzer reveals what is happening.

First we send the usual address frame and write the 0xE3. Then after a pause the read address frame is sent and the clock line is held low by the device (lower trace).

The clock line is held low by the device for over 42ms while it gets the data ready. It is released and the three data frames are sent:

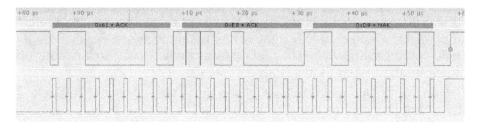

The second way of doing the job sends the command and gets the data in one operation:

```
mraa_i2c_read_bytes_data(i2c,0xE3,buf,3);
uint8_t msb= buf[0];
uint8_t lsb= buf[1];
uint8_t check= buf[2];
printf("msb %d \n lsb %d \n checksum %d \n",msb,lsb,check);
```

The only difference is that now there is no pause between sending the command 0xE3 and the read address frame. We still have to wait more than 42ms for the data, however.

Finally, we have to find out how to use the No hold master mode of reading the data as it is sometimes useful. In this case we can't use the single read_bytes_data command because the data will not be ready to read and the master will not be forced to wait for it. We have to use the two-step send the command and read the data approach:

```
mraa_i2c_write_byte(i2c,0xF3);
uint8_t buf[3];
while(mraa_i2c_read(i2c, buf, 3)==0){};
uint8_t msb= buf[0];
uint8_t lsb= buf[1];
uint8_t check= buf[2];
printf("msb %d \n lsb %d \n checksum %d \n",msb,lsb,check);
```

This polls repeatedly until the data is returned. Notice that the read function returns zero if it has failed to read data. The big difference is that now we could do some other work in the while loop until the data is returned.

Processing the Data

Our next task isn't really directly related to the problem of using the I2C bus, but it is a very typical next step. The device returns the data in three bytes, but the way that this data relates to the temperature isn't simple.

If you read the data sheet you will discover that the temperature data is the 14-bit value that results by putting together the most and least significant bytes and zeroing the bottom two bits. The bottom two bits are used as status bits – bit zero currently isn't used and bit one is a 1 if the data is a humidity measurement and a 0 if it is a temperature measurement. To put the two bytes together we use:

```
unsigned int data16=
    ((unsigned int) msb << 8)|(unsigned int) (lsb & 0xFC);
```

This zeroes the bottom two bits, shifts the msb up eight bits and ORs the two together. The result is a 16-bit temperature value with the bottom two bits zeroed. Now we have raw temperature value but we have still have to convert it to standard units. The datasheet gives the formula

```
Temp in C = -46.85 + 175.72 * data16 / 216
```

The only problem in implementing this is working out 2^{16}. You can work out 2^x with the expression $1<<x$ i.e. shift 1 x places to the right. This gives:

```
float temp =(float)(-46.85 + (175.72*data16/(float)
(1<<16)));
```

Of course, 2^{16} is a constant that works out to 65536 so it is more efficient to write:

```
float temp =(float)(-46.85 + (175.72*data16/(float)65536));
```

It is worth noting that the floating point arithmetic provided by the Edison makes all this calculation very much easier than it would be on a small 8-bit microcontroller. The final program is:

```
int main()
{
 mraa_i2c_context i2c;
 i2c = mraa_i2c_init(1);
 mraa_i2c_address(i2c, 0x40);
 uint8_t data =mraa_i2c_read_byte_data (i2c, 0xE7);
 printf("Register= %d \n", data);uint8_t buf[3];
 mraa_i2c_read_bytes_data(i2c,0xE3,buf,3);
 uint8_t msb= buf[0];
 uint8_t lsb= buf[1];
 uint8_t check= buf[2];
 printf("msb %d \n lsb %d \n checksum %d \n",msb,lsb,check);
 unsigned int data16=((unsigned int) msb << 8) |
                        (unsigned int) (lsb & 0xFC);
 float temp = (float)(-46.85+(175.72 * data16/(float)65536));
 printf("Temperature %f C \n",temp);
 return MRAA_SUCCESS;
```

```
}
```

Reading the Humidity

The good thing about I2C and using a particular I2C device is that it gets easier. Once you have seen how to do it with one device the skill generalizes and once you know how to deal with a particular device other aspects of the device are usually similar. To read the humidity we can more or less use the same program, we just need to change the command and the formula for the final percentage humidity.

The command needed to read the three data bytes is 0xE5 and the formula to convert the 16-bit value to percentage humidity is:

```
RH= -6 + 125 * data16 / 2^16
```

Putting all this together and reusing some variables from the previous program we have:

```
mraa_i2c_read_bytes_data(i2c,0xE5,buf,3);
msb= buf[0];
lsb= buf[1];
check= buf[2];
printf("msb %d \n lsb %d \n checksum %d \n",msb,lsb,check);
data16=((unsigned int) msb << 8) |(unsigned int) (lsb & 0xFC);
float hum = (float)(-6 + (125.0 * data16 / (float)65536));
printf("Humidity %f %% \n",hum);
```

The only unusual part of the program is using %% to print a single % character, which is necessary because % means something in printf.

Checksum Calculation

Although computing a checksum isn't specific to I2C, it is another common task.

The datasheet explains that the polynomial used is:

```
X8+X5+X4+1
```

Once you have this information you can work out the divisor by writing a binary number with a one in each location corresponding to a power of X in the polynomial,i.e. the 8th, 5th, 4th and 1st bit. Hence the divisor is 0x0131.

What you do next is roughly the same for all CRCs. First you put the data that was used to compute the checksum together with the checksum value as the low order bits:

```
uint32_t data32 =((uint32_t)msb << 16)|((uint32_t)lsb <<8)|
                                        (uint32_t) check;
```

Now you have three bytes, i.e 24 bits, in a 32-bit variable.

Next you adjust the divisor so that its most significant non-zero bit aligns with the most significant bit of the three bytes. As this divisor has a one at bit eight it needs to be shifted 15 places to the right to move it to be the 24th bit:

```
uint32_t divisor = ((uint32_t) 0x0131) <<15;
```

Now that you have both the data and the divisor aligned, you step through the top-most 16 bits, i.e. you don't process the low order eight bits which is the received checksum. For each bit you check to see if it is a one – if it is you replace the data with the data XOR divisor. In either case you shift the divisor one place to the right:

```
for (int i = 0 ; i < 16 ; i++){
 if( data32 & (uint32_t)1<<(23 - i) ) data32 =data32 ^ divisor;
 divisor=divisor >> 1;
};
```

When the loop ends, if there was no error, the data32 should be zeroed and the received checksum is correct and as computed on the data received.

A complete function to compute the checksum with some optimizations is:

```
uint8_t crcCheck(uint8_t msb, uint8_t lsb, uint8_t check){
 uint32_t data32 = ((uint32_t)msb << 16)|((uint32_t) lsb <<8)
                                    | (uint32_t) check;
 uint32_t divisor = 0x988000;
 for (int i = 0 ; i < 16 ; i++){
  if( data32 & (uint32_t)1<<(23 - i) ) data32 ^= divisor;
  divisor>>= 1;
 };
 return (uint8_t) data32;
}
```

It is rare to get a crc error on an I2C bus unless it is overloaded or subject to a lot of noise.

Complete Listing

Including crc checks, the complete temperature and humidity program is:

```
#include "mraa.h"
#include <stdio.h>
#include <unistd.h>
uint8_t crcCheck(uint8_t, uint8_t, uint8_t);
int main()
{
 mraa_i2c_context i2c;
 i2c = mraa_i2c_init(1);
 mraa_i2c_address(i2c, 0x40);
 uint8_t data =mraa_i2c_read_byte_data (i2c, 0xE7);
 printf("Register= %d \n", data);
 uint8_t buf[3];
 mraa_i2c_read_bytes_data(i2c,0xE3,buf,3);
 uint8_t msb= buf[0];
 uint8_t lsb= buf[1];
```

```
uint8_t check= buf[2];
printf(" msb %d \n lsb %d \n checksum %d \n",msb,lsb,check);
printf("crc %d \n ", crcCheck(msb,lsb,check));
unsigned int data16=((unsigned int) msb << 8) |
                               (unsigned int) (lsb & 0xFC);
float temp = (float)(-46.85 + (175.72 * data16 / (float)65536));
printf("Temperature %f C \n",temp);
mraa_i2c_read_bytes_data(i2c,0xE5,buf,3);
msb= buf[0];
lsb= buf[1];
check= buf[2];
printf(" msb %d \n lsb %d \n checksum %d \n", msb,lsb,check);
printf("crc %d \n ", crcCheck(msb,lsb,check));
data16=((unsigned int) msb << 8) | (unsigned int) (lsb & 0xFC);
float hum = (float)(-6 + (125.0 * data16 / (float)65536));
printf("Humidity %f %% \n",hum);return MRAA_SUCCESS;
}

uint8_t crcCheck(uint8_t msb, uint8_t lsb, uint8_t check){
  uint32_t data32 = ((uint32_t)msb << 16)|((uint32_t) lsb <<8) |
                               (uint32_t) check;
  uint32_t divisor = 0x988000;
  for (int i = 0 ; i < 16 ; i++)
  {
    if( data32 & (uint32_t)1<<(23 - i) )data32 ^= divisor;
    divisor>>= 1;
  };
  return (uint8_t) data32;
}
```

Of course this is just the start. Once you have the device working and supplying data it is time to write your code in the form of functions that return the temperature and the humidity and generally make the whole thing more useful and easier to maintain.

This is often how this sort of programming goes. At first you write a lot of inline code so that it works as fast as it can then you move blocks of code to functions to make the program more elegant and easy to maintain checking at each refactoring that the programming still works.

Summary

1. The SparkFun HTU21D is a good first I2C device to work with on the Edison because it will work at 1.8V

2. It can be used in polling or hold master mode – both work.

3. Once you have the raw data there is usual an additional step to convert it into meaningful data

4. Computing a checksum is also a common way to check for errors.

One of the big problems with using the Edison, or so many believe, is that in its "raw" form it works with 1.8V logic. In practice this isn't as big a problem as you might imagine. Often you don't have to do anything and when you do it is an easy and cheap fix.

When you use the Edison with the Arduino breakout board then there are logic level converters that save you from having to worry about this issue. However, to make the best use of the Edison then you need to use the mini-breakout board which doesn't buffer or level shift its raw GPIO lines. This means that you either have to find sensors and transducers that work with 1.8V logic or you have to implement level shifters of your own. Once you have done this a few time it becomes very easy and is very cheap.

The following descriptions of how things work are aimed at the reader who knows some basic physics - Ohm's Law say - but isn't an electronics expert.

Logic Levels

All logic implementation have a range of voltages that are regarded as a zero and a one. These are important specifications that you need to know to make sure that your implementation of logic or logic level shifting works in a wide range of situations. The diagram below summarizes the logic levels for the most commonly encountered systems.

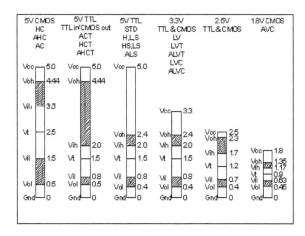

In each case the important numbers are Vih, Vil, Voh and Vol, which give you the voltage range the inputs and outputs work with. For example, for 1.8V logic Vih and Vil are 1.17V and 0.63V. That is, if the input is 1.17V or greater it reads a one and if it is 0.63 or lower it reads a zero. The Voh and Vol figures give you the limits on the outputs of the logic family. For 1.8V logic Voh is 1.35 and Vol is 0.45. What this means is that any 1.8V device will output at least 1.35V for a one and at most 0.45V for a zero.

You can see that these figures give you a margin of tolerance. If the output is low then it will be at most 0.45V and this is below the 0.63V needed by Vil, which therefore reads it as zero. The Edison specification gives Vil as 0.35*Vdd and Vol as 0.45V, which is exactly the standard as long as Vdd is 1.8V.

Of course your level shifters and custom logic aim for 1.8V for a one and 0V for a zero, but the logic voltage levels tell you how accurate you have to be and what you can expect from the standard logic in the worst case.

Output 1.8V To 3.3V and 5V

For output level conversion the key figures are Voh and Vol. The GPIO line will be at least 1.35V when high and not more than 0.45V for a low.

As we are talking about voltage levels there is a tendency to immediately think that a voltage controlled device such as a MOSFET is the obvious choice. However the difficulty is finding a MOSFET with a gate threshold voltage in the correct range. Most general purpose MOSFETs have too high a threshold voltage to be turned on by 1.8V.

Even if you find a MOSFET with a gate threshold voltage of 1.8V, on average it is not going to be turned on sufficiently by the 1.8V on the GPIO line. In the worst case the GPIO line might be as low as 1.3V and the MOSFET gate threshold could be 2V or more. Also note that the gate threshold is the minimum voltage need to make the MOSFET just start to conduct.

There are specially made N Channel MOSFETs for use in 1.8V logic circuits, for example, the FDN327B. Its characteristics are:

VGS(th) Gate Threshold Voltage min 0.4 avg 0.7 max 1.5 V

Equally important is the figure:

RDS(ON) = 120 mΩ @ VGS = 1.8 V

which is the resistance at a gate voltage of 1.8V. A typical MOSFET has a higher on resistance at its quoted gate threshold voltage. You can see that in this case it is low enough to conduct a reasonable current at 3.3V or 5V.

Any MOSFET that you plan to use for a 1.8V level converter has to have parameters similar to or better than the FDN327B.

One big problem with the 1.8V MOSFETs is that they are generally surface mount components. This is not a huge problem in that in many case this is exactly what you want, but it does make prototyping more difficult. If you want to use such MOSFETs then your choices are to buy a device pre-mounted on a breakout board, use a general purpose breakout board, or solder some wires to the surface mount contacts.

A good alternative to a MOSFET is an "old fashioned" Bipolar Junction Transistor, BJT. The BJT often gets left out of introductory electronics courses because it is a current controlled device and this is more difficult to understand and work with. However in this case it has a big advantage. If you think of the silicon BJT as a simple 3-terminal switch, then it switches on when the base reaches 0.6V relative to the emitter. If you compare this to the 1.8V logic thresholds you can see that it is a good fit and, what is more, any silicon npn transistor works in this way. That is, you can use almost any general purpose npn transistor to convert 1.8V logic to 3.3V or 5V logic.

In the rest of this chapter the 2N2222 transistor is used because it is common, cheap and available in a range of packages including through-hole, making it easy to use for prototyping.

Output Level Conversion

The most basic level converter has been introduced in earlier chapters. but it is worth repeating:

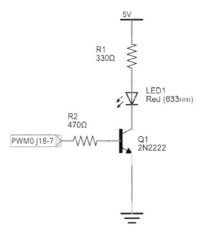

When the Edison's output line is high the transistor conducts and there is approximately 0.6V between the base and the emitter and hence 1.8-0.6=1.2V across R2.

First, let's assume that the output line is set to the default output mode strong, i.e. active pull up and active pull down. The output line can provide 3mA so the smallest value of R2 you should use is 400ohms, i.e. 1.2/0.003. Although the diagram shows a value of 470ohms, you can use higher values to limit the current to lower values.

Given that the 2N2222 always has a current gain of more than 50, if you put all the output current I into the base then the load can have up to 50*I mA. In this example this is roughly 150mA. In practice, the load would take less than this because its current is limited by R1.

The voltage drop across the transistor can be ignored as it is a few tenths of a volt, it is as if the LED is connected to ground when the transistor is full on. A red LED typically has a voltage drop of 2V and a working current of 10-20mA - this is why we don't try to drive an LED directly from the 3mA limited output line. Thus the voltage across R1 is 5-2=3V and the target current is 10mA giving R1=3/10*1000=300ohms minimum.

The same circuit works with 3.3V. The only change needed is in the value of the load resistor. Again assuming the LED drops 2V and works at a current of 10mA then R1=(3.3-2)/10*1000= 130ohms.

In general, if you want to drive a current load. simply find the current I you want to flow through it that voltage V that is across it at that current - look it up in a data sheet. Then the load resistor that you need is:

R1=(Vs-V)/I ohms.

where Vs is the supply voltage - 5V and 3.3V in the two cases above.

Things are a tiny bit more complicated when the load is a voltage load. A voltage load simply wants to be connected to a varying voltage and doesn't pass very much current - it is a high impedance load. In this case you don't put the load in series with the load resistor, but connect it to the load resistor as shown:

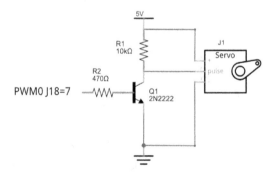

This is the servo circuit introduced in Chapter 7. The pulse input to the servo is a high impedance voltage input. In this case R1 simply acts to limit the voltage through the transistor. At 10K ohms the current through the transistor is at most 0.5 mA. As long as the connection to the servo or any voltage load only takes a small current compared to this 0.5 mA you can ignore the load and consider the voltage across R1 to vary from zero to 5V. Changing the supply voltage to 3.3V simply lowers the current though the transistor and R1.

The problem with this circuit is that, as far as the voltage is concerned, it is inverting. If the Edison's output line is low then the transistor is cut off and the pulse line is effectively connected to 5V via R1. When the line is high the the transistor is fully on and the voltage on the pulse line is zero as it is effectively connected to ground though the transistor.

Hence:

Edison line high = pulse line low

and vice versa.

Notice that this is a problem even if you replace the BJT with a MOSFET.

In the previous chapter we solved this problem with software and inverted the way the line was driven. Sometimes, because you are using third party software say, this is not possible.

The standard way of getting a non-inverting voltage converter is to use two transistors:

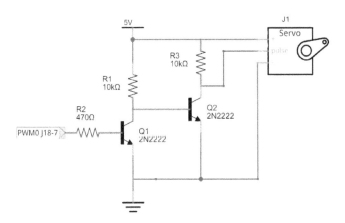

This works well but there is an easy way to do the same job with a single transistor - although it does have some limitations.

In this variation on a common base mode the transistor's base is connected to 1.8V and its collector to the 5V supply. If the Edison output is low then the base emitter voltage is 1.8V and the transistor is hard on, pulling the output to the servo low. If the Edison output is high the base emitter voltage is zero and the transistor is cut off, making the output to the servo high.

You can see that this is non-inverting, but the problem is that the current that flows through R2 is also the emitter current, which is the current the Edison I/O line has to sink. What this means is that the current in R2 is limited to around 2mA and this circuit provides no amplification. Of course you could

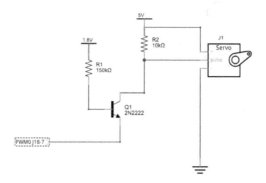

add another transistor to provide current amplification but in this case you would be better off going back to the standard 2-transistor arrangement.

This circuit does, however, work with most servos so in this role it is useful. If you are going to try it out with the servo program from the chapter on pulse width modulation, remember to change the timings to drive it in a non-inverted way. Both circuits also work at 3.3V.

5V and 3.3V to 1.8V input

Going from high to low logic for input is very easy. All you need are two resistors to form a potential divider. V is the input from the external logic and Vout it the connection to the Edison's input line.

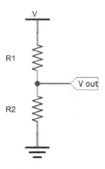

You can spend a lot of time on working out good values of R1 and R2. For loads that take a lot of current you need R1+R2 to be small and divided in the same ratio as the voltages. For most uses a total of 5K (or even 10K) is good enough. If V=5V then R1=3.3K and R2=1.8K work well. For V=3.3V, R1=2.7K and R2=2.2K work well.

The problem with a resistive divider is that it can round off fast pulses due to the small capacitive effects. This usually isn't a problem, but if it is then the solution is to use a transistor buffer again.

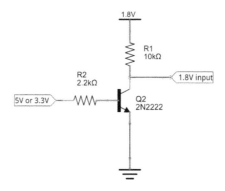

The role of R2 is simply to limit the input current taken from the output of the 5V or 3.3V device. The current is V-0.6/R2 where V is 5 or 3.3.

Notice that this is an inverting buffer but you can usually ignore this and simply correct in software, i.e. read a 1 as a low and a 0 as a high state.

In most case you should try the simple voltage divider and only move to an active buffer if it doesn't work.

Bi-directional Bus

The biggest problem in converting from 1.8V to 3.3 or 5V is when you need to work with a bi-directional bus.

There are, roughly speaking, three types of bi-directional bus: wire or, wire and, and tristate.

The most commonly encountered is the wire or, aka open collector, bus. This is used for I2C and many other 1-wire serial buses. The key idea is that the bus line is connected to a voltage reference via a resistor, generally a pull up resistor. This allows any device connected to the bus to ground it and so pull the bus line down. If more than one device pulls the bus down then no harm is done. However, the bus line only pulls up when all of the connected devices are inactive and allow the bus to drift up.

In the diagram below each of the switches represents a device connected to the bus. In practice the switches would be an active device such as a BJT or an FET but the principle is the same. You can see that closing any one of the switches grounds the pull up resistor which places the bus in low state.

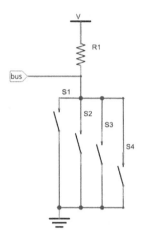

If you need to connect a 3.3V or 5V open collector bus to a 1.8V Edison input then you can make use of a chip designed to do the job but in many cases a simple classic single-transistor level shifter can do the job. For conversion to 3.3V you will often see an FET used but for the low voltage involved in a 1.8V conversion a BJT does the job very well.

This assumes that the output line is in pull up or open collector mode – see Chapter 15. The default for the mini-breakout board is strong i.e. push-pull mode. However, as long as the Edison is the only device on its side, i.e. 1.8V side of the bus, this still works.

For example:

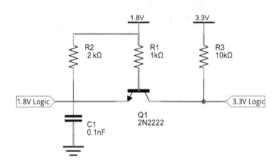

In practice R2 can have any value from 1K to 5K and R3 any from 5K to 10K depending on what is being driven. Notice that this assumes that the GPIO pin is in open collector mode with an external pull up resistor. In practice 2K is a good choice for R2.

To understand how this works we have to consider what happens when each side of the bus is pulled low. If the 1.8V logic input is pulled low then the emitter of the transistor is grounded and as the base is at 1.8V the transistor switches on and saturates so pulling the 3.3 logic bus down. The more difficult situation is when the 3.3V logic input is pulled low. In this case the collector is grounded and the base being at 1.8V puts the transistor into reverse active mode, i.e. with collector and emitter swapping roles. In this mode the transistor is still a current amplifier but with a much reduced gain (hfe). Given sufficient drive current, however, the transistor will still saturate and hence pull the 1.8V logic side of the bus low.

The reason for the capacitor is that, as the transistor changes operational mode, there is a charge storage effect which causes the voltage to suddenly drop, an effect you can see clearly:

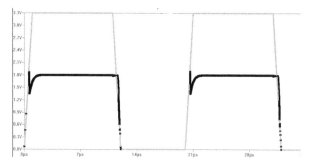

The gray trace is the 3.3V input signal and the black trace is the 1.8V output. In practice the undershoot can cause the Edison to detect two pulses in place of one.

With a small capacitance in place the effect is reduced:

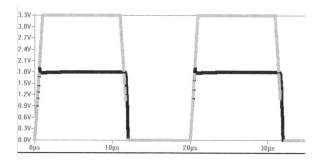

Notice that, as in the case of the single-transistor non-inverting buffer, the big problem is that there is no current amplification. When the Edison pulls the bus low it has to sink the current through R1, R2 and R3. The same is true on the 3.3V side, but in this case the total current is less than 1.5mA. The circuit works just as well at 5V with a slightly higher current.

You might expect the Edison's side of the bus needs to be driven with an open collector which is not the default mode – push-pull is. In fact it doesn't make any difference if the Edison is the only device driving the 1.8V logic input.

You can use an active high/active low drive as long as the Edison is the only device driving the bus and then the line is changed to an input to read the response from the responding device. If the output line drives the bus both high and low then a problem only arises when the slave attempts to drive the bus in the opposite direction. In most cases the slave doesn't attempt to drive the bus at the same time as the master and so the type of drive is irrelevant as long as the line reverts to input as soon as a slave starts transmitting data. However, it takes time to convert an output line to an input and this can be an additional problem.

Converting other types of bus follow the same general idea, but are more difficult.

You can build the circuit using a prototyping board or you can built it in-situ on the device you need to convert. Something like:

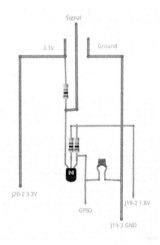

where the device in question is connected to the three wires at the top of the diagram.

This circuit is used in the next two chapters to interface bidirectional pull up buses.

Summary

1. There are 1.8V logic devices that will work directly with the Edison, but in many cases level shifting to 3.3 or 5V is needed to work with many popular sensors.

2. You can use IC level shifters, but a MOSFET or a BJT is often simpler if you don't want to convert many GPIO lines.

3. Finding a suitable MOSFET for 1.8V to 3.3 or 5V conversion is much harder than finding a BJT that will do the job – in fact almost any BJT will work.

4. A single stage common collector level shifter is inverting – sometimes this can be allowed for in software.

5. You can create a single stage common base level shifter that is not inverting, but you don't get any amplification.

6. Converting from 5 or 3.3V to 1.8V is usually easy to do with a passive voltage divider – if speed is an issue you might need to use a transistor level shifter.

7. A single BJT or MOSFET can be used to level shift in an open collector bus.

Chapter 11

Using the DHT11/22 Temperature Humidity Sensor at 1.8V

In this chapter we make use of all of the ideas introduced in earlier chapters to create a raw interface with the low cost DHT11/22 temperature and humidity sensor. It is an exercise in interfacing two logic families and implementing a protocol directly in C.

The Device

The DHT22 used in this project is a more accurate version of the DHT11, but the hardware and software will work with both versions and with the AM2302, which is similar to the DHT22.

```
Model AM2302/DHT22
Power supply 3.3-5.5V DC
Output signal digital signal via 1-wire bus
Sensing element Polymer humidity capacitor
Operating range
  humidity 0-100%RH;
  temperature -40~80Celsius
Accuracy
 humidity +-2%RH(Max +-5%RH);
 temperature +-0.5Celsius
Resolution or sensitivity
 humidity 0.1%RH;
 temperature 0.1Celsius
Repeatability
 humidity +-1%RH;
 temperature +-0.2Celsius
```

So the device will work at 3.3V and it makes use of a 1-wire open collector bus which will need to be converted to a 1.8V bus to work with the Edison. Unfortunately, the 1-wire bus isn't standard and is only used by this family of devices, so we have little choice but to implement the protocol in C.

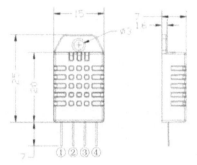

The pinouts are:

1. VDD
2. SDA serial data
3. not used
4. GND

and the standard way of connecting the device is:

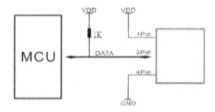

The serial protocol is also fairly simple:

- The host pulls the line low for between 0.8 and 29 ms, usually 1ms
- It then releases the bus which is pulled high
- After between 20 and 200 microseconds, usually 30 microseconds, the device starts to send data by pulling the line down for around 80 microseconds and then lets float high for another 80 microseconds.
- Next 80 bits of data are sent using a 70 microsecond high for a 1 and a 26 microsecond high for a zero the high pluses are separated by around 50 microsecond low period.

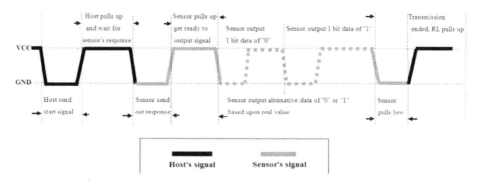

Host's signal   **Sensor's signal**

So what we have to do is pull the line low for 1ms or so to start the device sending data and this is very easy. Then we have to wait for the device to pull the line down and let it pull up again - about 160 microsecond and then read the time that the line is high 80 times.

A one corresponds to 70 microseconds and a zero corresponds to 26 microseconds. This is within the range of pulse measurement that can be achieved using fast memory mapped I/O. There is also a 50 microsecond period between each data bit and this can be used to do some limited processing. Notice that we are only interested in the time that the line is held high.

The Electronics

To convert the 3.3V device to work with the 1.8V Edison we can make use of the single-transistor level shifter introduced in the previous chapter:

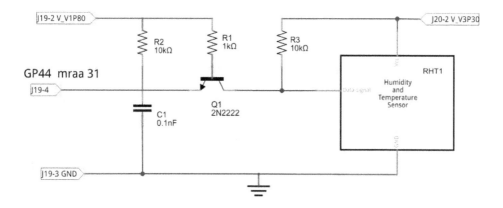

The pins used on the Edison connector are:

Mraa Number	Physical Pin	Edison Pin (SYSFS)
29	J19-2	V_V1P80
30	J19-3	GND
31	J19-4	GP44
43	J20-2	V_V3P30

It is worth recalling that for the mini-board you can't alter the output mode of a line using mraa. By default the output mode is push-pull. We really should change this to open collector but as the GPIO line reverts to an input any time that the sensor is driving the bus there isn't a problem with them both trying to drive the bus at the same time.

If you use a 2N2222 transistor then the pinouts are:

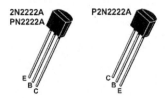

You can build the circuit on a prototype board to test the software but it is also fairly easy to build a free standing circuit on the DHT22 effectively converting it to 1.8V operation:

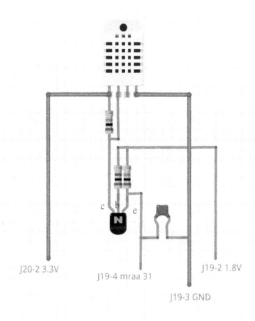

Isolate the components from one another using heat shrink sleeving. Of course the disadvantage is that now we have a four lead device and the cable cannot be as long - if it is long remove the capacitor as the lead will provide more capacitive loading than you need.

The Software

With the hardware shown above connected to the Edison the first thing that we need to do is establish that the system is working - just a little.

The simplest way to do this is to pull the line down for 1ms and see if the device responds with a stream of pulses. These can be seen on a logic analyzer or an oscilloscope - both are indispensable tools.

If you don't have access to either tool then you will just have to skip to the next stage and see if you can read in some data.

The simplest program that will do the job is:

```
int main()
{
 mraa_gpio_context pin = mraa_gpio_init(31);
 mraa_gpio_use_mmaped(pin,1);
 mraa_gpio_dir(pin, MRAA_GPIO_OUT_HIGH);
 mraa_gpio_write(pin, 0);
 usleep(1000);
 mraa_gpio_dir(pin, MRAA_GPIO_IN);
 return MRAA_SUCCESS;
}
```

Setting the line initially high we then set it low, wait for 1000 microseconds and then change its direction to input ready to read the data.

Notice that we don't have to set the mode of the output line as it can drive its side of the bus safe in the knowledge that the device will not try to drive it until it releases the low state and changes to a high impedance input.

As long as the circuit has been correctly assembled and you have a working device you should see something like:

Notice that the pulling low of the line actually lasts 1.3ms which is a bit on the long side but does no harm.

If you haven't used the capacitor in the level shifting circuit then you might see some of the pulses on the Edison's side look something like:

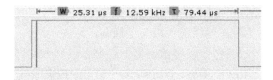

This is caused by the change in operating mode of the transistor. The capacitor acts as a high pass filter and smooths the glitch out. You might not see this effect even without the capacitor because often the circuit layout provides enough stray capacitance to smooth things out. Too much capacitance and the rise time of the pluses is compromised.

Reading the Data

With preliminary flight checks complete, it is time to read the 40-bit data stream. When doing this there are two things to keep in mind. The first is that it is only the time the line is high that matters and you need to measure just this accurately - you don't care so much about how long the line is low for. The second is that it is usually better to collect the bits and only later process them and extract the data. To this end it is usually a good idea to save the data in a buffer:

```
int buf[40];
int i;
int j;
for(j=0;j<=40;j++){
  for(i=1;i<200;i++){
   if(mraa_gpio_read(pin)==1)break;
  };
  for(i=1;i<200;i++){
   if(mraa_gpio_read(pin)==0)break;
  }
  buf[j]=i;
}
```

You should be able to see how this works.

The outer for loop repeats to read in all 41 bits, 40 data bits and the initial start bit. The inner loop waits for the line to go high and i gives the time that the line has been low. This is of no interest. Next the second for loop waits for the line to go low. The count in i is now proportional to the time the line was high and is stored in the buffer.

Complete Listing

That's all we need to do and the final program, complete with some minor tidying up can be seen below:

```
#include "mraa.h"
#include <stdio.h>
#include <unistd.h>

uint getByte(int,int[]);

int main()
{
 const struct sched_param priority={1};
 sched_setscheduler(0,SCHED_FIFO,&priority);

 mraa_gpio_context pin = mraa_gpio_init(31);
 mraa_gpio_use_mmaped(pin,1);
 mraa_gpio_dir(pin, MRAA_GPIO_OUT_HIGH);

 mraa_gpio_write(pin, 0);
 usleep(1000);
 mraa_gpio_dir(pin, MRAA_GPIO_IN);int buf[40];

 int i, j;
 for(j=0;j<=40;j++){
  for(i=1;i<200;i++){
   if(mraa_gpio_read(pin)==1)break;
  };
  for(i=1;i<200;i++){
   if(mraa_gpio_read(pin)==0)break;
  }
  buf[j]=0;
  if(i>75)buf[j]=1;
 }

 for(j=0;j<=40;j++){
  printf("%d %d \n",j,buf[j]);
 }

 int byte1=getByte(1,buf);
 int byte2=getByte(2,buf);
 int byte3=getByte(3,buf);
 int byte4=getByte(4,buf);
 int byte5=getByte(5,buf);

 printf("Checksum %d %d \n",byte5,
     (byte1+byte2+byte3+byte4) & 0xFF);

 float humidity= (float) (byte1<<8 |byte2)/10.0;
 printf("Humidity= %f \n",humidity);

 float temperature;
```

```
int neg=byte3&0x80;
byte3=byte3&0x7F;
temperature= (float) (byte3<<8 |byte4)/10.0;
if(neg>0)temperature=-temperature;
printf("Temperature= %f \n",temperature);

return MRAA_SUCCESS;
}

uint getByte(int b,int buf[]){
 int i;
 uint result=0;
 b=(b-1)*8+1;
 for(i=b;i<=b+7;i++){
  result<<=1;
  result |= buf[i];
 }
 return result;
}
```

Summary

1. The DHT22/11 is an example of a useful sensor which does not work at 1.8V

2. It is possible to interface it to the 1.8V logic using a single transistor.

3. The Edison in memory mapped I/O mode is fast enough to implement the custom protocol.

Chapter 12

The DS18B20 1-Wire Temperature

The Edison doesn't have built in support for the Maxim 1-Wire bus and this means you can't use the very popular DS18B20 temperature sensor. However, with a little careful planning you can and you can do it from user rather than kernel space.

The proprietary Maxim 1-Wire bus is very easy to use and enable you to connect a lot of useful devices including its iButton security devices. However, probably the most popular of all 1-wire devices is the DS18B20 temperature sensor which is small, very cheap and very easy to use, as long as the processor supports the 1-wire bus protocol. To overcome the fact that the Edison doesn't, the protocol is easy enough to program in C and the Edison is fast enough to work with it without needing anything extra, other than memory-mapped I/O.

The Hardware

The DS18B20 is available in a number of formats, but the most common makes it look just like a standard BJT, which can sometimes be a problem when you are trying to find one. You can also get them made up into waterproof sensors complete with cable.

No matter how packaged they will work at 3.3V or 5V but not at 1.8V without a level converter.

Its basic specification is:

- Measures Temperatures from -55°C to +125°C (-67°F to +257°F)
- ±0.5°C Accuracy from -10°C to +85°C
- Thermometer Resolution is User Selectable from 9 to 12 Bits
- Converts Temperature to 12-Bit Digital Word in 750ms (Max)

It can also be powered from the data line, making the bus physically need only two wires - data and ground. However, this "parasitic power" mode is difficult to make work reliably and best avoided in an initial design.

In normal powered mode there are just three connections:

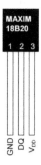

Ground needs to be connected to the system ground, VDD to 3.3V and DQ to the pullup resistor of an open collector bus.

There can be multiple devices on the bus and each one has a unique 64bit lasered ROM code which can be used as an address to select the active devices. For simplicity it is better to start off with a single device and avoid the problem of enumerating the devices on the bus, although once you know how everything works this isn't difficult to implement.

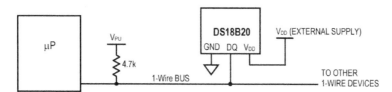

As we only have a single bus master, the Edison, and a single slave device, the DS18B20, we can use the same single-transistor level shifter introduced in earlier chapters. However there is an additional problem we have to solve, fast switching between input and output.

In the previous chapter we were able to implement the serial protocol because essentially the Edison sent the device a pulse and then the device did all the talking. This allowed the use of a single GPIO line. Initially it was set to output and used to send a pulse, then switched to input mode ready to read the 40 bits of data.

The problem is that changing between output and input mode is done using the SYSFS drivers and is comparatively slow - 15 to 20 microseconds. Fortunately, in the example of the DHT22, where the result of this slow transition was simply to miss part of the acknowledge pulse and the Edison was ready to read data well before the device started to send it.

In the case of the 1-wire bus things are very different. The master has to send a fast pulse on the line for every bit received and it has to be able to read the response in 15 microseconds. This is too fast to allow for time to change the line from output to input in time to read the data. However, given the specification of the 1-wire bus, it might be possible most of the time with some devices.

A more secure solution that should work with all 1-wire bus devices is to use two GPIO lines - one set to output, the other to input. This works because it eliminates the need to change the line's direction, but it does mean that you need to use two GPIO lines to drive the 1-wire bus. As long as you can afford this doubling up of GPIO lines then the solution works well.

The schematic of the level shifter and the DS18B20 is the same as for the circuit used in the previous chapter with the DS18B20 replacing the DHT22 and a second GPIO line connected.

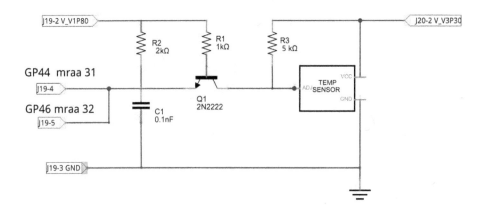

The pullup resistor R2 can be supplied by the Edison and if you opt to use its internal pullup you can omit R2 from the hardware. In the rest of the chapter is it assumed that R2 is present in the sensor and not supplied by the Edison. When you are first trying things out it is worth using a prototype board, but this level shifter can be assembled in place on the DS18B20 to effectively convert the sensor to 1.8V operation.

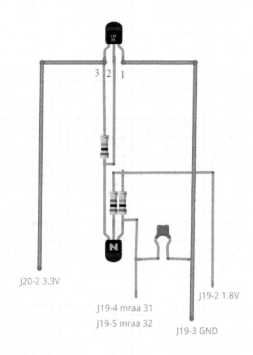

Again use heat shrink sleeving to avoid shorts between component wires. The disadvantage is that now we need four wires back to the Edison whereas only three are needed for a 3.3V device:

Initialization

Every transaction with a 1-wire device starts with an initialization handshake. First we have to get the GPIO lines set up correctly:

```
mraa_gpio_context pinIn;
mraa_gpio_context pinOut;
int main()
{
 const struct sched_param priority={1};
 sched_setscheduler(0,SCHED_FIFO,&priority);

 pinIn = mraa_gpio_init(32);
 mraa_gpio_use_mmaped(pinIn,1);
 mraa_gpio_dir(pinIn, MRAA_GPIO_IN);
 pinOut = mraa_gpio_init(31);
 mraa_gpio_use_mmaped(pinOut,1);
 mraa_gpio_dir(pinOut, MRAA_GPIO_OUT_HIGH);
```

This simply sets mraa line 32 to input and 31 to output. We also set a real-time priority to the entire program. This isn't really necessary as only the bit read/write functions are actually time critical, as will be explained later.

Also notice that the variables, pinIn and pinOut, have been made file level, i.e. global, so that they don't have to be passed to the functions that make use of them. In practice you can refactor this code to make them parameters if you want to create a more general 1-wire library.

We also need the output line to be set to open collector. You cannot do this using mraa but it is easy enough to do via SYSFS as explained in Chapter 15. You have two choices - to use the internal 2K pullup resistor or use an external resistor. In this example we use an external resistor. Using the functions given in Chapter 15 we can set the output line to open collector/no pullup resistor using:

```
        putSetting(44,"pullmode","nopull");
        putSetting(44,"opendrain","enable");
```

Notice that GPIO-44 corresponds to mraa pin 31. If you don't include these two function calls the bidirectional bus will not work. For completeness the putSetting function is:

```
void putSetting(int pin,char prop[],char value[]){
 char buf[200];
 sprintf(buf, "/sys/kernel/debug/gpio_debug/
                       gpio%d/current_%s",pin,prop);
 int fd = open(buf, O_WRONLY);
 write(fd, value, strlen(value));
 close(fd);
}
```

Now we have to send the initialization pulse, which is simply a low pulse that lasts at least 480 microseconds. A 15 to 60 microsecond pause follows and then any and all of the devices on the bus pull the line low for 60 to 240 microseconds.

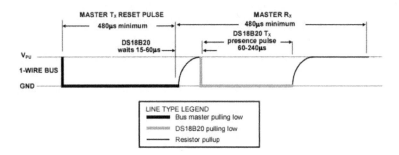

This is fairly easy to implement as a function:

```
int init(){
 mraa_gpio_write(pinOut, 0);
 usleep(500);
 mraa_gpio_write(pinOut, 1);
 usleep(60);
 int b=mraa_gpio_read(pinIn);
 usleep(500);
 return b;
}
```

We pull the line low for 500 microseconds and then let it be pulled back up. After a 60-microsecond wait, which is right at the start of the guaranteed period when the line should be low if there is an active device on the bus, we read the input line and then wait another 500 microseconds to complete the data slot.

As this is such a slow and inaccurate transaction it makes sense to use usleep rather than a busy wait loop. It releases control back to the OS so that some other program can run but it usually creates a pause that is longer than the time specified. Hence if there is a device the function should return zero and if there are no devices it should return a one:

```
if(init()==1){
 printf("No device \n");
 return MRAA_SUCCESS;
}
```

If you try this partial program and have a logic analyzer you will see something like:

The actual initialization pulse is 567 microseconds and after a pause of 30 microsecond the device pulls the bus low for 110 microseconds in response. These timings can vary, but a little over 90 microseconds after the end of the initialization pulse should always be within the presence pulse.

Seeing a presence pulse is the simplest and quickest way to be sure that your hardware is working.

Writing Bits

Our next task is to implement the sending of some data bits to the device.

The 1-wire bus has a very simple data protocol. All bits are sent using a minimum of 60 microseconds for a read/write slot. Each slot must be separated from the next by a minimum of 1 microsecond. The good news is that timing is only critical within each slot. You can send the first bit in a time slot and then take your time before you send the next bit - the device will wait for you. This means you only have to worry about timing within the functions that read and write individual bits.

- To send a zero you have to hold the line low for most of the slot.

- To send a one you have to hold the line low for just between 1 and 15 microseconds and leave the line high for the rest of the slot.

The exact timings can be seen below;

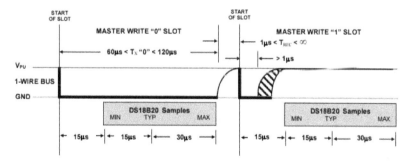

It seems reasonable to use the typical timings shown on the diagram. So for a zero we hold the line low for 60 microsecond then let it go high for the remainder of the slot. To send a one we hold the line for a bit more than 1 microsecond and then let it go high for the remainder of the slot.

So our sendZero function is:

```
void sendZero(){
 int i;
 mraa_gpio_write(pinOut, 0);
 for(i=1;i<4000;i++){};
 mraa_gpio_write(pinOut, 1);
 for(i=1;i<60;i++){};
}
```

and our sendOne function is:

```
void sendOne(){
 int i;
 mraa_gpio_write(pinOut, 0);
 for(i=1;i<60;i++){};
 mraa_gpio_write(pinOut, 1);
 for(i=1;i<4000;i++){};
}
```

Notice that the functions keep control after letting the line go high again. In principle they could return and let the main program do some processing, but this would mean that the main program had to hold off sending another bit until the 60 microseconds was up. This approach isn't efficient, but it is simple. Also notice that as the time periods are short and they have to be fairly repeatable a busy wait is the best option for the delay.

With these constants the measured pulse widths are:

- For a zero the line is held low for just over 60 microseconds with a pause of about 1.5 microseconds
- For a one the line is held low for 1.5 microseconds and the slot is about 60 microseconds in total

As the only time critical operations are the actual setting of the line low and then back to high, there is no need to worry too much about speed of operation of the entire function. So we might as well combine the two functions into a single writeBit function:

```
void writeBit(int b){
 int i,delay1,delay2;
 if(b==1){
  delay1=60;delay2=4000;
 }else{
  delay1=4000;delay2=60;
 }
 mraa_gpio_write(pinOut, 0);
 for(i=1;i<delay1;i++){};
 mraa_gpio_write(pinOut, 1);
 for(i=1;i<delay2;i++){};
}
```

The code at the start of the function simply increases the time between slots slightly.

You can see a one followed by a zero in the following logic analyzer trace:

A First Command

After discovering that there is at least one device connected to the bus, the master has to issue a ROM command. In many cases the ROM command used first will be the Search ROM command which enumerates the 64-bit codes of all of the devices on the bus. After collecting all of these codes the master can used the Match ROM commands with a specific 64-bit code to select the device the master wants to talk to.

While it is perfectly possible to implement the Search ROM procedure, it is simpler to work with the single device by using commands which ignore the 64-bit code and address all of the devices on the bus at the same time. Of course this only works as long as there is only one device on the bus.

If there is only one device then we can use the Skip ROM command 0xCC to tell all the devices on the bus to be active. As we already have a writeBit function this is easy:

```
void sendskip(){
 writeBit(0);
 writeBit(0);
 writeBit(1);
 writeBit(1);

 writeBit(0);
 writeBit(0);
 writeBit(1);
 writeBit(1);
}
```

Notice that 0xCC is 1100 1100 in binary and the 1-wire bus sends the least significant bit first.

If you try this out you should find it works but device doesn't respond because it is waiting for another command. Again as the time between writing bits isn't critical we can take this first implementation of the function and write something more general if slightly slower.

The writeByte function will write the low 8 bits of an int to the device:

```
void writeByte(int byte){
int i;
 for(i=0;i<8;i++){
  if(byte & 1){
   writeBit(1);
  }else{
   writeBit(0);
  }
  byte=byte>>1;
 }
}
```

Using this we can send a Skip ROM command using:

```
writeByte(0xCC);
```

You can see the pattern of bits sent by the Edison on a logic analyzer:

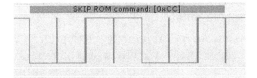

Reading Bits

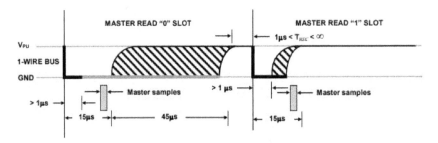

We already know how the master sends a one and a zero. The protocol for the device is exactly the same except that the master still provides the starting pulse of the slot. That is, the master starts a 60-microsecond slot by pulling the bus down for a bit more than 1 microsecond. Then the device either holds the line down for a minimum of a further 15 microseconds, or it simply allows the line to float high. See below for the exact timings:

So all we have to do to read bits is to pull the line down for just a bit more than 1 microsecond and then sample the bus at the end of a 15-microsecond pause.

```
int readBit(){
 int i;
 mraa_gpio_write(pinOut, 0);
 for(i=1;i<60;i++){};
 mraa_gpio_write(pinOut, 1);

 for(i=1;i<800;i++){};
 int b= mraa_gpio_read(pinIn);
 for(i=1;i<3500;i++){};
 return b;
}
```

The readBit function pulls the line low for about 1.5 microseconds and measures the line state at around 12.5 microseconds. The total slot time is around 630 microseconds. Again, it is better to use busy waits as the time periods are short and need to be repeatable.

A logic analyzer shows the typical pattern of bits from the device:

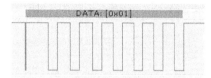

The narrow initial low pulse corresponding to a one slot is 1.5 microseconds and the longer low pulses corresponding to a zero slot is 28 microseconds with the slot lasting 690 microseconds.

After using the program for a lot of measurements, it turns out a loop time of 450 iterations reduces the error rate considerably. It seems earlier is better.

Initiating A Temperature Conversion

Our next task is to send a Convert command 0x44. This starts the DS18B20 making a temperature measurement. Depending on the resolution selected this can take as long as 750ms. How the device tells the master that the measurement has completed depends on the mode it is operating in but using an external power line, i.e. not using parasitic mode, the device sends a zero bit in response to a bit read until it is completed when it sends a 1.

As we already have a readBit function this is easy. The software polls for the completion by reading the bus until it gets a 1 bit:

```
int convert(){
 int i;
 writeByte(0x44);
 for(i=1;i<1000;i++){
  usleep(10000);
  if(readBit()==1)break;
 };
 return (i==1000);
}
```

You can of course test the return value to check that the result has been obtained.

When the function returns, the new temperature measurement is stored in the devices scratchpad memory and now all we have to do is read this.

Reading the Scratchpad

The scratchpad memory has nine bytes of storage in total and does things like control the accuracy of conversion and provide status information. However, in our simple example the only two bytes of any great interest are the first two, which hold the result of a temperature conversion.

Before we move on to read the scratchpad we need a function that will read a byte. As in the case of writing a byte there is no time criticality in the time between reading bits so we don't need to take extra special care in constructing the function;

```
int readByte(){
 int byte=0;
 int i;
 for(i=0;i<8;i++){
  byte=byte | readBit()<< i;
 };
 return byte;
}
```

The only difficult part is to remember that the 1-wire bus sends the least significant bit first and so this has to be shifted into the result from the right.

Now we have a readByte function getting the data is simple. We have to issue a Read Scratchpad 0xBE command and then read the nine bytes that the device returns. However, to send the new command we have to issue a new initialization pulse and a Skip ROM 0xCC command followed by a read scratchpad command 0xBE:

```
if(init()==1){
 printf("No device \n");
 return MRAA_SUCCESS;
}
writeByte(0xCC);
writeByte(0xBE);
```

Now the data is ready to read. We can read all nine bytes of it or just the first two. The device will keep track of where the read is, so if you come back later and read more bytes you will get the first unread one. If you issue an initialization pulse then the device aborts the data transmission.

We need the first two bytes, the least and most significant bytes of the 11-bit temperature reading, as a 16-bit, 2-complement integer.

```
int b1= readByte();
printf("%d \n",b1);
int b2= readByte();
printf("%d \n",b2);
```

Getting the Temperature

All we now have to do do is to put the two bytes together as a 16-bit integer. As the Edison supports a 16-bit int we can do this very easily:

```
int16_t temp1= (b2<<8 | b1) ;
float temp= (float)temp1/16 ;
printf("temperature = %f C \n",temp);
return MRAA_SUCCESS;
}
```

Notice that this only works because int16_t really is a 16-bit integer. If you were to use:

```
int temp1= (b2<<8 | b1);
```

then temp1 would be correct for positive temperatures, but it would give the wrong answer for negative values because the sign bit isn't propagated into the top 16 bits. If you want to use a 32-bit integer then you will have to propagate the sign bit manually:

```
if(b2 & 0x80) temp1=temp1 | 0xFFFF0000;
float temp= (float)temp1/16;
```

Now we have a basic program to read the temperature and some useful 1-wire functions. The next task would be to refactor more of the code to create a function that reads the temperature on demand. Once you have the basic bit read/write functions the rest follows fairly easily. Missing from the program given below is the ability to write to the configuration register to select the resolution, but in most cases 12-bit the default is what you want.

Also missing is the CRC calculation to check for errors and most important of all the enumeration algorithm that discovers what 1-wire devices are active on the bus. The CRC is important because you will encounter an incorrect result about one in every 50 to 100 readings for one reason or another. These omissions are fairly straightforward to provide now that we have the low-level data functions.

One advantage of a user mode implementation is that you can easily implement some of the functions that the kernel mode drivers often omit. You can also expand the operation to other 1-wire devices such as iButtons etc.

Complete Listing

```
#include "mraa.h"
#include <stdio.h>
#include <unistd.h>int init();

int readBit();
int readByte();
void writeBit(int);
void writeByte(int);
int convert();
void putSetting(int,char[],char[]);

mraa_gpio_context pinIn;
mraa_gpio_context pinOut;

int main() {
 const struct sched_param priority = { 1 };
 sched_setscheduler(0, SCHED_FIFO, &priority);

 pinIn = mraa_gpio_init(32);
 mraa_gpio_use_mmaped(pinIn, 1);
 mraa_gpio_dir(pinIn, MRAA_GPIO_IN);pinOut =

 mraa_gpio_init(31);
 mraa_gpio_use_mmaped(pinOut, 1);
 mraa_gpio_dir(pinOut, MRAA_GPIO_OUT_HIGH);
putSetting(44,"pullmode","nopull");
putSetting(44,"opendrain","enable");

 if (init() == 1) {
  printf("No device \n");
  return MRAA_SUCCESS;
 }
 writeByte(0xCC);
 convert();

 if (init() == 1) {
  printf("No device \n");
  return MRAA_SUCCESS;
 }
 writeByte(0xCC);
 writeByte(0xBE);

 int b1 = readByte();
 printf("%d \n", b1);
 int b2 = readByte();

 printf("%d \n", b2);
 int16_t temp1 = (b2 << 8 | b1);
 float temp = (float) temp1 / 16;
 printf("temperature = %f C \n", temp);
 return MRAA_SUCCESS;
```

```
}

void writeBit(int b) {
 int i;
 int delay1, delay2;
 if (b == 1) {
  delay1 = 60;
  delay2 = 4000;
 } else {
  delay1 = 4000;
  delay2 = 60;
 }
 mraa_gpio_write(pinOut, 0);
 for (i = 1; i < delay1; i++) {
 };
 mraa_gpio_write(pinOut, 1);
 for (i = 1; i < delay2; i++) {
 };
 }

int readBit() {
 int i;
 mraa_gpio_write(pinOut, 0);
 for (i = 1; i < 60; i++) {
 };
 mraa_gpio_write(pinOut, 1);
 for (i = 1; i < 450; i++) {
 };
 int b = mraa_gpio_read(pinIn);
 for (i = 1; i < 3500; i++) {
 };
 return b;
}

void writeByte(int byte) {
 int i;
 for (i = 0; i < 8; i++) {
  if (byte & 1) {
   writeBit(1);
  } else {
   writeBit(0);
  }
  byte = byte >> 1;
 }
}

int readByte() {
 int byte = 0;
 int i;
 for (i = 0; i < 8; i++) {
  byte = byte | readBit() << i;
 };
 return byte;
}
```

```
int convert() {
 int i;
 writeByte(0x44);
 for (i = 1; i < 1000; i++) {
  usleep(10000);
  if (readBit() == 1)
   break;
  };
 return (i == 1000);
}

int init() {
 mraa_gpio_write(pinOut, 0);
 usleep(500);
 mraa_gpio_write(pinOut, 1);
 usleep(60);
 int b = mraa_gpio_read(pinIn);
 usleep(500);
 return b;
}
void putSetting(int pin,char prop[],char value[]){
 char buf[200];
 sprintf(buf, "/sys/kernel/debug/gpio_debug/
                 gpio%d/current_%s",pin,prop);
 int fd = open(buf, O_WRONLY);
 write(fd, value, strlen(value));
 close(fd);
}
```

Summary

1. Implementing a 1-wire bus protocol in a C program is possible.

2. You can use the usual bidirectional level conversion techniques but you have to change the mode of the output line to open collector.

3. To avoid having to wait while a single GPIO line changes its direction we have to use two GPIO lines – one for input and one for output.

The SPI bus can be something of a problem because it doesn't have a well defined standard that every device conforms to. Even so, if you only want to work with one specific device it is usually easy to find a configuration that works - as long as you understand what the possibilities are.

SPI Bus Basics

The SPI bus is commonly encountered as it is used to connect all sorts of devices from LCD displays, through realtime clocks, to AtoD converters. It is also used for high data rate streaming, for example, getting video data from a camera.

The SPI bus is strange because there is no standard for it and different companies have implemented it in different ways, which means that you have to work harder to implement it in any particular case. However, it usually works, which is a surprise for a bus with no standard or clear specification.

The reason it can be made to work is that you can specify a range of different operating modes, frequencies and polarities. This makes the bus slightly more complicated to use, but generally it is a matter of looking up how the device you are trying to work with implements the SPI bus and then getting the Edison to work in the same way.

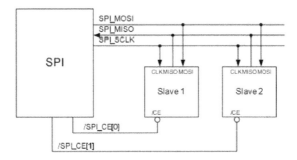

The bus is odd in another way - it does not use bidirectional serial connections. There is a data line for the data to go from the master to the slave and a separate data line from the slave back to the master. That is, instead of a single data line that changes its transfer direction, there is one for data out and one for data in. There is a variation on the SPI bus that does use a bidirectional mode where a single wire is used for the data, but the Edison doesn't support this. It is also worth knowing that the drive on the SPI bus is push-pull and not open collector/drain. This provides higher speed and more noise protection as the bus is actively driven high and low.

You can see the sort of configuration that the Edison expects. There is a single master and at most two slaves. The signal lines are:

- MOSI Master Output Slave Input, i.e. data to the slave
- MISO Master Input Slave Output, i.e. data to the master
- SCLK Serial Clock, which is always generated by the master

There can also be any number of SS (Slave Select) and CE (Chip Enable, or in Edison's terminology Chip Select) lines, which are usually set low to select which slave is being addressed.

Notice that unlike other buses, I2C for example, there are no SPI commands or addresses, only bytes of data. However, slave devices do interpret some of the data as commands to do something or send some particular data.

The Edison has only a single SPI bus exposed on the mini-breakout board and only two SS lines. This means that in principle you can only connect two SPI devices. In practice mraa only uses CS1 and so you can only connect a single slave device. This can be overcome by using GPIO lines as chip select lines and/or using CS0 directly.

The pins that are used for the Edison's SPI bus are:

MRAA Number	Physical Pin	Edison Pin (SYSFS)	Pinmode0	Pinmode1
9	J17-10	GP111	GPIO-111	SPI-5-CS1
10	J17-11	GP109	GPIO-109	SPI-5-SCK
11	J17-12	GP115	GPIO-115	SPI-5-MOSI
23	J18-10	GP110	GPIO-110	SPI-5-CS0
24	J18-11	GP114	GPIO-114	SPI-5-MISO
29	J19-2	V_V1P80		
30	J19-3	GND		
43	J20-2	V_V3P30		

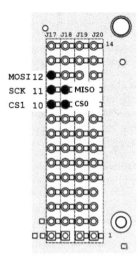

The data transfer on the SPI bus is also slightly odd. What happens is that the master pulls one of the chip selects low which activates a slave. Then the master toggles the clock SCLK and both the master and the slave send a single bit on their respective data lines. After eight clock pulses a byte has been transferred from the master to the slave and from the slave to the master.

You can think of this as being implemented as a circular buffer - although it doesn't have to be.

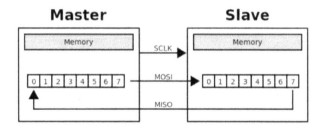

This full duplex data transfer is often hidden by the software and the protocol used. For example, there is a read function that reads data from the slave and sends zeros or data that is ignored by the slave. Similarly there is a write function that sends valid data, but ignores whatever the slave sends. The transfer is typically in groups of eight bits and usually most significant bit first, but this isn't always the case. In general, as long as the master supply clock pulses data is transferred.

Notice this circular buffer arrangement allows for slaves to be daisy chained with the output of one going to the input of the next. This makes the entire chain one big circular shift register. This can make it possible to have multiple devices with only a single chip select, but it also means any commands sent to the slaves are received by each one in turn. For example you could send a convert command to each AtoD converter in turn and receive back results from each one.

The final odd thing about the SPI bus is that there are four modes which define the relationship between the data timing and the clock pulse. The clock can be either active high or low - clock polarity CPOL and data can be sampled on the rising or falling edge of the clock - clock phase CPHA. All combinations of these two possibilities gives the four modes:

SPI Mode*	Clock Polarity CPOL	Clock Edge CPHA	Characteristics
0	0	0	Clock active high data output on falling edge and sampled on rising
1	0	1	Clock active high data output on rising edge and sampled on falling
2	1	0	Clock active low data output on falling edge and sampled on rising
3	1	1	Clock active low data output on rising edge and sampled on falling

*The way that the SPI modes are labeled is common but not universal.

There is often a problem trying to work out what mode a slave device uses. The clock polarity is usually easy and the Clock phase can sometimes be worked out from the data transfer timing diagrams and:

- First clock transition in the middle of a data bit means CPHA=0
- First clock transition at the start of a data bit means CPHA=1

So, to configure the SPI bus to work with a particular slave device you must:

1. Select the clock frequency - anything from 125MHz to 3.8KHz
2. Set the CS polarity - active high or low
3. Set the clock mode Mode0 thru Mode3

Now we have to find out how to do this using the mraa library.

The SPI Functions

There are thee functions concerned with enabling and disabling the SPI bus:

- `mraa_spi_init (int bus)`
- `mraa_spi_stop (mraa_spi_context dev)`
- `mraa_spi_init_raw (unsigned int bus, unsigned int cs)`

Initialization

Before you make use of the SPI bus you have to initialize it using:

```
mraa_spi_context dev SPI=mraa_spi_init (0)
```

This returns the SPI context if successful and NULL otherwise. After this the pins allocated to the SPI bus no longer work as general purpose GPIO pins.

When you are finished using the SPI bus you can return the pins to general GPIO lines by calling:

```
mraa_spi_stop (SPI)
```

You can also use mraa to initialize a bus without any board configuration using mraa_spi_init_raw, but this isn't something you generally want to do as the basic init doesn't do any initialization if it recognizes that it is working with the mini-breakout board.

Configuration

There are a number of functions that you can use to configure the way the bus works:

- `mraa_spi_frequency (mraa_spi_context dev, int hz)`
- `mraa_spi_mode (mraa_spi_context dev, mraa_spi_mode_t mode)`
- `mraa_spi_lsbmode (mraa_spi_context dev, mraa_boolean_t lsb)`
- `mraa_spi_bit_per_word(mraa_spi_context dev,unsigned int bits)`

The frequency sets the speed of data transfer in Hz. For example:

```
mraa_spi_frequency (dev, 50000)
```

sets the bus frequency to 50kHz. The theoretical maximum speed is 25MHz but in the current implementation the SPI bus doesn't always work at the speed you set.

mraa_spi_mode can be used to set the data transfer to one of:

MRAA_SPI_MODE0	CPOL = 0, CPHA = 0, Clock idle low, data is clocked in on rising edge, output data (change) on falling edge
MRAA_SPI_MODE1	CPOL = 0, CPHA = 1, Clock idle low, data is clocked in on falling edge, output data (change) on rising edge
MRAA_SPI_MODE2	CPOL = 1, CPHA = 0, Clock idle low, data is clocked in on falling edge, output data (change) on rising edge
MRAA_SPI_MODE3	CPOL = 1, CPHA = 1, Clock idle low, data is clocked in on rising, edge output data (change) on falling edge

You can also set the bit order and number of bits in each data transfer:

```
mraa_spi_lsbmode (dev,TRUE)
mraa_spi_bit_per_word(dev,8)
```

This sets the bit order to least significant bit first and 8-bit transfers. The lsbmode function seems to have no effect in the current version of mraa. Notice that bit_per_word only affects data transferred in word units if it is in the range 16 or less and byte transfers if it is 8 or less.

That is:

- If you try to send a byte and specify 10 bits - nothing happens.
- If you try to send a word and specify 10 bits - only 10 bits are sent.
- If you specify 5 bits and send a byte - only the low order 5 bits are sent.

You can't specify more than 16 bits for the transmission of a word.

Although some of the examples in the documentation use the SPI without configuring it, i.e. accepting the defaults, this isn't a good idea. If you do accept the defaults you can find that the bus behaves erratically and incorrectly, for example with no clock pulse.

Always set the bus to reasonable values such as:

```
mraa_spi_mode (spi, MRAA_SPI_MODE0 );
mraa_spi_frequency(spi, 400000);
mraa_spi_lsbmode(spi, 0);
mraa_spi_bit_per_word(spi,8);
```

Data transfer functions

Because of the way the SPI bus uses a full duplex transfer things are a little different from other buses when it comes to implementing functions to transfer data. If you recall that the data transfer sends a byte of data out of the register while shifting in a byte of data then the transfer functions will make sense:

- `mraa_spi_write(mraa_spi_context dev,uint8_t data)`
- `mraa_spi_write_word(mraa_spi_context dev,uint16_t data)`
- `mraa_spi_write_buf(mraa_spi_context dev,uint8_t *data,`
                                              `int length)`
- `mraa_spi_write_buf_word(mraa_spi_context dev,uint16_t *data,`
- ` `   `int length)`
- `mraa_spi_transfer_buf(mraa_spi_context dev,uint8_t *data,`
                            `uint8_t *rxbuf, int length)`
- `mraa_spi_transfer_buf_word (mraa_spi_context dev,`
              `uint16_t *data,uint16_t *rxbuf, int length)`

The most basic of this set of functions is **write** which sends a single byte to the slave while receiving a single byte sent back. Unlike the underlying protocol it doesn't overwrite the original value with the slave's data.

So, to send and receive data, you would use something like:

```
uint8_t Send_data=0x55;
int Read_data;
Read_data = mraa_spi_write(dev,Send_data);
```

Of course, you can always simply throw away the data from the slave if you just want a "write" or send meaningless data to the slave if you just want a "read".

You can specify how many bits are sent using bit_per_word. For example:

```
mraa_spi_bit_per_word(spi,5);
uint8_t Send_data=0x55;
int Read_data;
Read_data = mraa_spi_write(dev,Send_data);
```

will only send the low-order 5 bits.

The **write_word** function works in the same way as **write** but it sends a word containing up to 16 bits without deactivating the CS line. You can use bit_per_word to specify exactly how many bits are sent.

For example:

```
mraa_spi_bit_per_word(spi,14);
uint16_t trans=0xF000;
uint16_t recv = mraa_spi_write_word(spi,trans );
```

transfers the low order 14 bits in trans to recv. In this case this means that recv will contain 0x3000. Not many SPI devices work with anything other than 8 bits.

The remaining functions all send multiple bytes of data stored in a buffer. They differ in how they return the data and each one comes in a byte or a word version. The byte versions always send 8 bits at a time and the word versions send anything up to 16 bits.

Let's look at each one in turn. The first two send a buffer of data and return a pointer to a buffer of data received. There is a byte version:

- mraa_spi_write_buf (dev,data, length)

and a word version:

- mraa_spi_write_but_word (dev, data, length)

The difference is that in the byte version data is a byte array and in the word version it is a 16-bit array. Again, the word version will send the number of bits from each word as set by bit_per_word. For example:

```
uint8_t buf[]={0x01,0x02,0x03};
uint8_t *read =mraa_spi_write_buf (spi, buf, 3);
```

sends three bytes and receives three bytes without deactivating the CS line. It is your responsibility to free up the buffer that the function returns.

The final two functions work in exactly the same way but with the difference that the received data is stored in a buffer of your choice:

- `mraa_spi_transfer_buf (dev, data[],rxbuf[], length)`

- `mraa_spi_transfer_buf_word (dev, data[],rxbuf[], length)`

For example:

```
uint8_t buf[]={0x01,0x02,0x03};
uint8_t recv[3];
mraa_spi_transfer_buf (spi, buf, recv,3);
```

sends three bytes and receives three bytes, but now into an array that you have created in your program.

Using just these functions you should be able to deal with most SPI slaves. Now we come to a subtle point. What is the difference between transferring multiple bytes using write_buf or transfer_buf and simply sending the bytes individually using multiple write calls?

The answer is that each time you make a write call the chip select line is activated, the data is transferred and then it is deactivated. When you use buffer transfers the chip select is left active for the entire transfer, i.e. it isn't deactivated between each byte. Sometimes this difference isn't important and you can transfer three bytes using three calls to **transfer** or one call to **tranfernb**. However, some slaves will abort the current multibyte operation if the chip select line is deactivated in the middle of a multibyte transfer.

It is important to realize that the nature of the transfer is that the first byte is sent at the same time that the first byte is received. That is, unlike other protocols, the whole of the send buffer isn't sent before the received data comes back. The whole transfer works a byte at a time - the first byte is sent while the first byte is being received, then the second byte is sent at the same time the second byte is being received and so on. Not fully understanding this idea can lead to some interesting bugs.

A Loop Back Example

Because of the way that data is transferred on the SPI bus it is very easy to test that everything is working without having to add any components. All you have to do is connect MOSI to MISO so that anything sent it also received in a loop back mode.

First connect pin J17/12 to pin J18/11 using a jumper wire and start a new project.

The program is very simple. First we initialize the SPI bus:

```
mraa_spi_context spi = mraa_spi_init(0);
```

As this is a loop back test we really don't need to configure the bus, but for completeness:

```
mraa_spi_mode (spi, MRAA_SPI_MODE0 );
mraa_spi_frequency(spi, 400000);
mraa_spi_lsbmode(spi, 0);
mraa_spi_bit_per_word(spi,8);
```

Next we can send some data and receive it right back:

```
uint16_t read_data = mraa_spi_write(spi,0xAA);
```

The hex value AA is useful in testing because it generates the bit sequence 10101010, which is easy to see on a logic analyzer.

We can check that the received data matches the sent data in a variety of ways:

```
if( read_data== 0xAA)printf("data received correctly");
```

Finally we close the bus and the library:

```
mraa_spi_stop(spi);
return MRAA_SUCCESS;
```

Putting all of this together gives us the complete program:

```
#include "mraa.h"
#include <stdio.h>
#include <unistd.h>int main() {
 mraa_spi_context spi = mraa_spi_init(0);
 mraa_spi_mode(spi, MRAA_SPI_MODE0);
 mraa_spi_frequency(spi, 400000);
 mraa_spi_lsbmode(spi, 0);
 mraa_spi_bit_per_word(spi, 8);
 uint16_t read_data = mraa_spi_write(spi, 0xAA);
 if (read_data == 0xAA) printf("data received correctly");
 mraa_spi_stop(spi);
 return MRAA_SUCCESS;
}
```

If you run the program and don't got the "data received correctly" message then the most likely reason is that you have connected the wrong two pins together or not connected them at all.

Some Edison SPI Problems

If you connect a logic analyzer to the four pins involved - J17-10,11 and 12 and J18-11 - you will see the data transfer:

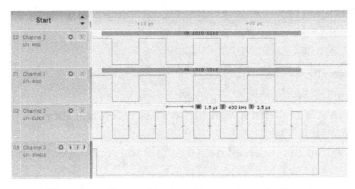

If you look carefully you will see the CS0 line go low before the master places the first data bit on the MOSI and hence on the MISO lines. Notice that the clock rises in the middle of each data bit making this a mode 0 transfer. You can also see that the clock is measured to be 400KHz as promised.

All as expected. However if you change the program to repeatedly send a single byte of data:

```
for (;;) {
 uint16_t read_data = mraa_spi_write(spi, 0xAA);
}
```

you will see something you might not have expected:

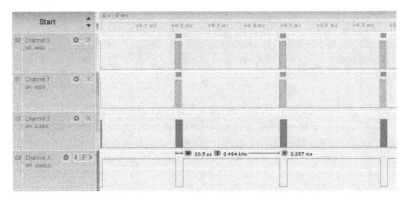

The clock rate may be specified as 400KHz, but the data rate is much slower. There is a 0.26ms delay between each byte transferred. The delay effectively reduces the data rate to just less than 4.5K bytes/s from its theoretical upper limit of 50K bytes/s.

What this means is that the data rate isn't as dependent on the clock speed as you might expect:

Clock speed	Transfer rate
1MHz	5K bytes/s
400KHz	4.49K bytes/s
200KHz	3.8K bytes/s
100KHz	3.24K bytes/s
50KHz	2.43K bytes/s
10KHz	0.83K bytes/s

The reason for this behavior is simply the overhead in calling the SPI functions to send a single byte.

Earlier versions of Yocto Linux showed the same data transfer rates, but the slowdown was achieved by putting a delay in after the CS line had been activated. You might think that the way to get a higher data rate is to use one of the buffer transfer functions which don't toggle the CS line between each byte or word and which run the clock continuously. However, if you try this with Yocto Linux 3 you will find that its behavior is a little strange.

For example, the program:

```
for (i = 0; i < 1000; i++)
 buf[i] = i;
uint8_t recv[1000];
int n = 1000;
mraa_result_t res= mraa_spi_transfer_buf(spi,buf,recv,n);
for (i = 0; i < n; i++) {
 if (recv[i] != buf[i])
   printf("error %d , %d,%d \n", recv[i], buf[i], i);
}
```

transfers 1000 bytes containing 0,1,2,3,4 and so on and then compares the received data.

You will find that you get error messages for all values after the first if the clock frequency is lower than about 800KHz. If you reduce the number of bytes sent to three or fewer then it does work. If you use a clock frequency of 800KHz to less than 1MHz then it works but the clock speed is less than set.

At 1MHz it works correctly and the clock speed is 1MHz with occasional pauses giving a data transfer rate of around 0.125Mbytes/s. At 2Mhz it is 0.26Mbytes/s , 10MHz gives 1.6Mbytes/s and at 25MHz the transfer rate is 3.12Mbytes/s. However you have to keep the buffer size to less than around 5Kbytes or there are overrun errors.

The latest version of the SPI driver has changed to make use of DMA data transfer - hence the much higher speeds achievable. If you select a clock speed lower than 1MHz then the DMA seems to get out of sync with the bus.

The documentation also says:

- In a single-frame transfer, the SoC supports all four possible combinations for the serial clock phase and polarity.
- In multiple frame transfer, the SoC supports SPH=1 and SPO= 0 or 1.
- The SoC may toggle the slave select signal between each data frame for SPH=0

This means that multiple frame transfers only support Modes 1 and 3 and the CS line my be toggled between frames in modes 0 and 4. In practice this doesn't seem to happen.

A User Mode Driver

The SPI bus doesn't seem able to do data transfers with a clock much slower than 1MHz. This is good for fast devices such as video displays, but some devices can't work this fast. If you need to transfer multiple blocks of data the speed also drops due to the gaps between function calls. There is also the problem of supporting more SPI devices than the Edison hardware supplies.

We can solve some of these problems with a software emulation of the SPI bus.

The good news is that the SPI protocol is very simple. We will implement a mode 0 transfer of a single byte. The code presented is very simple and you could improve it a lot at the cost of clarity and perhaps, if you are not careful, speed.

The SPI protocol in mode 0 with CS active low and SCK active high is:

1. Set CS1 to 0 wait a short time
2. Put the data out on MOSI
3. Wait 1 full delay
4. Set SCK to 1
5. Read MISO
6. Wait 1 full delay
7. Set SCK to 0
8. Send all eight bits - repeat 2 to 7 - and then set CS1 to 1 again.

You can see that we are setting the data just after the falling edge of the clock and reading the data just after the rising edge.

Implementing the User Mode Driver

In principle the two delays could be different to allow for a difference between a slaves setup and hold time. In practice we generally select the longest delay. Notice that most SPI devices don't demand that the clock pulses are of the same length so we don't have to worry about being accurate.

As long as you are using version 3 of the IoT software you can make use of the same lines as the Edison's SPI bus to implement your own. Before version 3 you couldn't use all of the SPI bus lines as GPIO lines because they were used in the Linux Kernel.

To get started first we need to define some global variables:

```
mraa_gpio_context CS0;
mraa_gpio_context SCK;
mraa_gpio_context MOSI;
mraa_gpio_context MISO;
```

If you want to tidy things up these could be placed into a struct and passed as a single parameter. You could then use the struct to set up any four GPIO lines as an SPI bus.

The function that we are going to create is:

```
uint8_t sendbyte(uint8_t byte, int delay);
```

This sends byte and returns the byte received. The delay parameter sets the clock frequency.

We could have a function to initialize the GPIO lines to work as an SPI bus but for the moment let's just put them in the main program:

```
int main() {
```

First we set up the program to run in a FIFO scheduling group. This should make it the only program to run until it gives up control, see Chapter 6 for more information.

```
const struct sched_param priority = { 1 };
sched_setscheduler(0, SCHED_FIFO, &priority);
```

Next we initialize each of the SPI lines in turn:

```
CS1 = mraa_gpio_init(9);
mraa_gpio_dir(CS1, MRAA_GPIO_OUT);
mraa_gpio_use_mmaped(CS1, 1);
mraa_gpio_write(CS1, 1);
SCK = mraa_gpio_init(10);
mraa_gpio_dir(SCK, MRAA_GPIO_OUT);
mraa_gpio_use_mmaped(SCK, 1);
mraa_gpio_write(SCK, 0);
MOSI = mraa_gpio_init(11);
mraa_gpio_dir(MOSI, MRAA_GPIO_OUT);
mraa_gpio_use_mmaped(MOSI, 1);
mraa_gpio_write(MOSI, 0);
MISO = mraa_gpio_init(24);
mraa_gpio_use_mmaped(MISO, 1);
mraa_gpio_dir(MISO, MRAA_GPIO_IN);
mraa_gpio_read(MISO);
```

The only thing that you might wonder about is the final read of the MISO line. Why bother? The answer is that the first read takes longer than subsequent reads because the pin is setup at this point. So a gratuitous read, throwing the result away, speeds up the first byte transfer. It is always a good idea to read an input line when you first set it up.

Now we need to implement the function we can return to the main program in a moment. We need two loop variables and a byte variable to read the data in:

```
uint8_t sendbyte(uint8_t byte, int delay) {
  int i, j;
  int read=0;
```

Now we are all set to send eight bits one bit at a time. First we set the CS1 line low to select the slave, then we need a short pause to give the slave time, and then we can start the loop that sends each of the bits:

```
mraa_gpio_write(CS1, 0);
for (j = 1; j < 100; j++) {
};
for (i = 0; i < 8; i++) {
```

We need to set the data line high or low depending on the most significant bit in byte:

```
mraa_gpio_write(MOSI, byte & 0x80);
```

and then we need to shift the entire bit pattern one to the left to get the next bit into the most significant bit position:

```
byte = byte << 1;
```

Now we busy wait, the only way to wait that doesn't return control to the operating system, for half a clock period and then set the clock high:

```
for (j = 1; j < delay; j++) {
};
mraa_gpio_write(SCK, 1);
```

Next we need to read the data on MISO. This is the most significant bit and it needs to be shifted one place to the left to ensure it eventually gets to the correct position:

```
read = read << 1;
read = read | (mraa_gpio_read(MISO));
```

Notice that the first shift doesn't actually do anything but its easier to put up with this waste than to waste even more time trying to test to eliminate it.

Next we wait for another half a clock period and then set the clock low.

```
for (j = 1; j < delay-10; j++) {
};
mraa_gpio_write(SCK, 0);}
```

This ends the loop that processes the eight bits and now all that remains is to deactivate the CS1 line and return the result.

```
mraa_gpio_write(CS1, 1);
for (j = 1; j < 20; j++) {
};
return (uint8_t) read;
}
```

Continuing with the main program from where we left off, we can now make use of the function to send and receive some data:

```
int delay = 0;
uint8_t read;
for(;;){
  read = sendbyte(0xAA, delay);
  if(read!=0xAA)printf("Error \n");
}
return MRAA_SUCCESS;
}
```

Assuming that the MISO and MOSI pins are connected together in a loop back, the output AA should equal the input AA.

If you run this and measure the clock frequency you will find it is around 666KHz and the data rate is 66K bytes/s. This is the fastest data transfer. Things can be slowed down by setting other values to delay:

Delay	Clock	Transfer
0	666KHz	66K bytes/s
10	500KHz	62K bytes/s
100	222KHz	26K bytes/s
200	133KHz	16K bytes/s
500	47KHz	7.2K bytes/s
1000	31KHz	3.8K bytes/s

Once you get to a delay of 500 or more you will discover that the delay after setting the CS1 line might not be enough. It really needs to be a percentage of the clock frequency. If you want to work down at these frequencies change the delay for CS1 to:

```
for (j = 1; j < delay/8+100; j++) {}
```

You can easily tidy up this function and program to produce something more like a library function. In addition you can modify it to create a buffer transfer function which works at similar speeds. An example of how to do this is given in the next chapter.

Notice that while data is being transferred the function hogs one core of the Edison main CPU and the rest of your program makes no progress. However, if you replace the busy waits by other instructions you do have time to perform some light processing of the input data.

The complete program is:

```c
#include "mraa.h"
#include <stdio.h>
#include <unistd.h>
uint8_t sendbyte(uint8_t byte, int delay);
mraa_gpio_context CS1;
mraa_gpio_context SCK;
mraa_gpio_context MOSI;
mraa_gpio_context MISO;

int main() {
 const struct sched_param priority = { 1 };
 sched_setscheduler(0, SCHED_FIFO, &priority);
 CS1 = mraa_gpio_init(9);
 mraa_gpio_use_mmaped(CS1, 1);
 mraa_gpio_dir(CS1, MRAA_GPIO_OUT);
 mraa_gpio_write(CS1, 1);
 SCK = mraa_gpio_init(10);
 mraa_gpio_use_mmaped(SCK, 1);
 mraa_gpio_dir(SCK, MRAA_GPIO_OUT);
 mraa_gpio_write(SCK, 0);
 MOSI = mraa_gpio_init(11);
 mraa_gpio_use_mmaped(MOSI, 1);
 mraa_gpio_dir(MOSI, MRAA_GPIO_OUT);
 mraa_gpio_write(MOSI, 0);
 MISO = mraa_gpio_init(24);
 mraa_gpio_use_mmaped(MISO, 1);
 mraa_gpio_dir(MISO, MRAA_GPIO_IN);
 mraa_gpio_read(MISO);
 int delay = 1000;
 uint8_t read;
 for (;;) {
  read = sendbyte(0xAA, delay);
  if (read != 0xAA)
  printf("Error \n");
 }
 return MRAA_SUCCESS;
}
uint8_t sendbyte(uint8_t byte, int delay) {
 int i, j;
 int read = 0;
 mraa_gpio_write(CS1, 0);
 for (j = 1; j < delay / 8 + 100; j++) {
 };
 for (i = 0; i < 8; i++){
```

```
mraa_gpio_write(MOSI, byte & 0x80);
byte = byte << 1;
for (j = 1; j < delay; j++) {
};
mraa_gpio_write(SCK, 1);
read = read << 1;
read = read | (mraa_gpio_read(MISO));
for (j = 1; j < delay; j++) {
};
mraa_gpio_write(SCK, 0);
}
mraa_gpio_write(CS1, 1);
for (j = 1; j < delay / 8 + 20; j++) { };
return (uint8_t) read;
}
```

General SPI Problems

The SPI bus is often a real headache because of the lack of a definitive standard, but in most cases you can make it work. The first problem is in discovering the characteristics of the slave device you want to work with. In general this is solved by a careful reading of the data sheet or perhaps some trial and error - see the next chapter for an example.

If you are working with a single slave then generally things work once you have the SPI bus configuration set correctly. Where things are more difficult is if you have multiple devices on the same bus. The Edison can only directly support two devices but this is enough to make the task more difficult. Typically you will find SPI devices that don't switch off properly when they are not being addressed. In principle all SPI devices should present high impedance outputs (i.e. tristate buffers) when not being addressed, but some don't. If you encounter a problem you need to check that the selected slave is able to control the MISO line properly.

A better solution is to multiplex the CS0/1 lines to create additional chip selects. For example, you can use standard GPIO lines as chip selects and connect more than two SPI slaves.

Summary

1. The SPI bus is often problematic because there is no SPI standard.

2. Unlike other serial buses it makes use of unidirectional connections.

3. The data lines are MOSI master output slave input and MISO master input slave output.

4. In addition there is a clock line - output from master; and an unspecified number of select lines - two in the case of the Edison.

5. Data is transferred from the master to the slave and from the slave to the master on each clock pulse in arranged as a circular buffer.

6. The mraa library provides all the functions you need to set up the SPI bus and transfer data one byte or multiple bytes at a time.

7. You can test the SPI bus using a simple loopback connection.

8. Working with a single slave is usually fairly easy, working with multiple slaves can be more of a problem.

9. In single byte transfers cannot achieve a high data rate because of the overheads involved in the mraa calls. In this case 5Kbytes/s is about as fast as you can achieve.

10. Multiple byte transfers can achieve higher data rates because the latest system software uses DMA but this only works with clock rates of 1MHz and higher. You can achieve data rates of 3Mbytes/s.

11. Multiple byte transfers are limited to blocks of around 5Kbytes.

12. You can achieve transfer rates of up to 65K byte/s using your own software implementation of the SPI protocol.

Chapter 14

SPI In Practice with the MCP3008 AtoD

The SPI bus can be difficult to make work at first, but once you know what to look for about how the slave claims to work it gets easier. To demonstrate how it is done let's add eight channels of 10-bit AtoD using the MCP3008.

The Edison with the mini-breakout board doesn't have any analog inputs or outputs. You could move up to the Arduino board, but this is physically large and overkill. A simpler solution is to interface an MCP3008 directly to the Edison's SPI bus. It is also a good example of working with the SPI bus.

The MCP3000 family of AtoD converters provides a simple and low cost alternative to fitting an entire expansion board. The MCP3004 and the MCP3008, with four and eight AtoD inputs at 10-bit precision respectively, are the best known, but there are others in the family, including 12-bit and 13-bit precision devices with differential inputs at around the same sort of cost or around $1 to $2.

In this chapter the MCP3008 is used because it is readily available and provides a good performance at low cost, but the other devices in the family work in the same way and could be easily substituted.

The MCP3008

The MCP3008 is available in a number of different packages, but the standard 16-pin PDIP is the easiest to work with using a prototyping board.

Its pinouts are fairly self-explanatory:

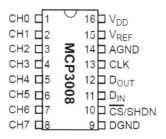

You can see that the analog inputs are on the left and the power and SPI bus connections on the right. The conversion accuracy is claimed to be 10 bits, but how many of these bits correspond to reality and how many are noise depends on how you design the layout of the circuit.

You need to take great care if you need high accuracy. For example, you will notice that there are two voltage inputs, VDD and VREF.

VDD is the supply voltage that runs the chip and VREF is the reference voltage that is used to compare the input voltage. Obviously if you want highest accuracy VREF, which has to be lower than or equal to VDD, should be set by an accurate low noise voltage source. However in most applications VREF and VDD are simply connected together and the usual, low-quality supply voltage is used as the reference. If this isn't good enough then you can use anything from a Zener diode to a precision voltage reference chip such as the TL431. At the very least, however, you should add a 1uF capacitor between the VDD pin and the VREF pin to ground.

The MC3000 family is a type of AtoD called a successive approximation converter. You don't need to know how it works to use it, but it isn't difficult. The idea is that first a voltage is generated equal to VREF/2 and the input voltage is compared to this. If it is less, the most significant bit is a zero; and if it is more than or equal to it then it is a one. At the next step the voltage generated is VREF/2 + VREF/4 and the comparison is repeated to generate the next bit.

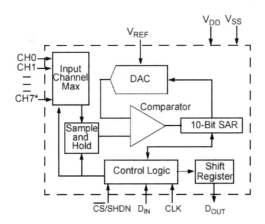

You can see that successive approximation fits in well with a serial bus as each bit can be obtained in the time needed to transmit the previous bit. However, the conversion is relatively slow and a sample and hold circuit has to be used to keep the input to the converter stage fixed. The sample and hold takes the form of a 20pF capacitor and a switch.

The only reason you need to know about this is that the conversion has to be complete in a time that is short compared to the discharge time of the capacitor - so for accuracy there is a minimum SPI clock rate as well as a maximum. Also, to charge the capacitor quickly enough for it to follow a changing voltage, it needs to be connected to a low-impedance source. In most cases this isn't a problem, but if it is you need to include an op amp.

If you are using an op amp buffer then you might as well implement a filter to remove frequencies from the signal that are too fast for the AtoD to respond to, an anti-aliasing filter. How all this works takes us into the realm of analog electronics and signal processing and well out of the core subject matter of this book.

You can also use the AtoD channels in pairs - differential mode - to measure the voltage difference between them. In differential mode you measure the difference between CH0 and CH1, i.e. what you measure is CH1 - CH0.
In most cases you want to use all eight channels in single-ended mode.

In principle, you can take 200K samples per second, but only at the upper limit of the supply voltage VDD=5V. This falls to 75K samples per second at its lower limit of VDD=2.7V.

The SPI clock limits are a maximum of 3.6MHz at 5V and 1.35MHz at 2.7V. The clock can go slower, but because of the problem with the sample and hold mentioned earlier it shouldn't go below 10kHz. How fast we can take samples is discussed later in this chapter.

Connecting MCP3008 to Edison

The lower voltage operating point isn't quite low enough to allow it to work with the 1.8V Edison GPIO lines. There are 1.8V AtoD converters but they are more expensive and only available in surface mount packages. You can use an IC voltage translator and, given that there are four lines to convert, this may well be a good choice. However, the four lines are unidirectional - three outputs and one input to the Edison - and so simple transistor and resistor voltage translators suffice.

One small problem is that a single-transistor common-emitter buffer inverts the signal. We could cope with this in software, but the SPI bus isn't easy to use in an inverted mode. However, if we use the user space driver given at the end of the previous chapter, then a simple inverting buffer could be used and corrected for in the software.

To use the mraa SPI functions we need a non-inverting level translator and this is most simply achieved using the common base buffer introduced in the previous chapter and a simple resistor voltage divider.

The connection to the Edison's SPI bus is simple and can be seen in the diagram.

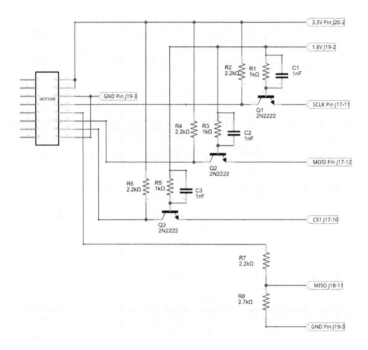

If you want to understand the way the level converter works take a look a just one of the transistor circuits:

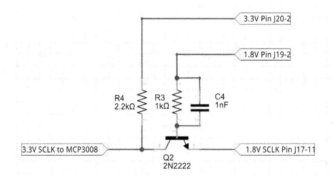

When the SCLK is low the transistor is on because the voltage difference between the base and emitter is 1.8V. Hence the output SCLK line is pulled low via the 1K resistor.

In this state the current in the Edison's GPIO line is roughly base current plus collector current:

```
base current = (1.8-0.6)V/1K = 1.2mA
collector current 3.2V/2.2K  = 1.45mA
```

or 2.65mA, which is below the 3mA the Edison can supply. You can increase the size of R4 but this reduces the high frequency performance.

When the SCLK goes high the voltage applied to the base is below the emitter voltage and the transistor is cut off. This allows R4 to pull the output high. In this mode state the current supplied by the Edison is negligible.

The only remaining component to explain is C4. This is a traditional "speed up" capacitor. Bipolar transistors take longer to switch off than switch on because of charge stored in the base region. The speed up capacitor provides charge to neutralize the base charge and so allows the transistor to switch off faster. A better alternative is to use a Schottky diode to stop the transistor going into deep saturation, but at the sort of speeds the Edison works at the capacitor is good enough.

The only additional component that is recommended is a 1uF capacitor connected between pins 15 and 16 to ground, mounted as close to the chip as possible. As discussed in the previous section, you might want a separate voltage reference for pin 15 rather than just using the 3.3V supply.

Basic Configuration

Now we come to the configuration of the SPI bus.

We have some rough figures for the SPI clock speed - 10kHz to a little more than 1.35MHz. So an initial clock frequency giving a frequency of 1MHz seems a reasonable starting point. This also means that the clock is in the region where the DMA transfer works correctly. However as we are only transferring three bytes the DMA works at lower frequencies.

From the data sheet the CS has to be active low and the most significant bit first is the default for both the master and the slave. The only puzzle is what mode to use?

This is listed in the data sheet if you look really carefully. It can be mode 0,0 with clock active high or mode 1,1 with clock active low. For simplicity we can use mode 0,0 which is mode0 in the bcm2835 library.

We now have enough information to initialize for the slave:

```
mraa_spi_context spi = mraa_spi_init(0);
mraa_spi_mode(spi, MRAA_SPI_MODE0 );
mraa_spi_frequency(spi,1000000);
mraa_spi_lsbmode(spi, 0);
mraa_spi_bit_per_word(spi,8);
```

The Protocol

Now we have the SPI initialized and ready to transfer data but what data do we transfer?

The SPI bus doesn't have any standard commands or addressing structure. Each device responds to data sent in different ways and sends data back in different ways. You simply have to read the data sheet to find out what the commands and responses are.

Reading the data sheet might be initially confusing because it says that what you have to do is send five bits to the slave - a start bit, a bit that selects its operating mode, single or differential, and a three-bit channel number.

The operating mode is 1 for single-ended and 0 for differential, so to read channel 3, i.e. 011, in single-ended mode you would send the slave:

```
11011xxx
```

where xxx means don't care. The response from the slave is that it holds its output in a high impedance state until the sixth clock pulse it then sends a zero bit on the seventh followed by bit 9 of the data on clock eight. That is the slave sends back:

```
xxxxxx0 b9
```

where x means indeterminate and b9 is zero or one depending on the data. The remaining nine bits are sent back in response to the next nine clock pulses. This means you have to transfer three bytes to get all ten bits of data. This all makes reading the data in eight-bit chunks confusing.

The data sheet suggests a different way of doing the job that delivers the data more neatly packed into three bytes. What it suggests is to send a single byte:

```
00000001
```

The slave transfers random data at the same time which is ignored. The final 1 is treated as the start bit. If you now transfer a second byte with most significant bit indicating single or differential mode, then a three-bit channel address and the remaining bits set to zero, the slave will respond with the null and the top two bits of the conversion. Now all you have to do to get the final eight bits of data is to read a third byte:

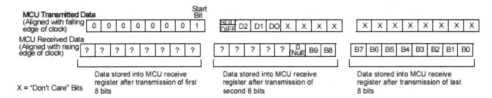

You can do it the first way that the data sheet describes, but this way you get two neat bytes containing the data with all the low-order bits in their correct positions.

Using this information we can now write some instructions that read a given channel. For example, to read channel zero we first send a byte set to 0x01 as the start bit and ignore the byte the slave transfers. Next we send 0x80 to select single-ended and channel zero and keep the byte the slave sends back as the high-order two bits. Finally we send a zero byte so that we get the low-order bits from the slave:

```
uint8_t buf[] = {0x01,0x80,0x00};
uint8_t readBuf[3];
mraa_spi_transfer_buf (spi, buf, readBuf,3);
```

Notice you cannot send the three bytes one at a time using transfer because that results in the CS line being deactivated between the transfer of each byte.

To get the data out of readBuf we need to do some bit manipulation:

```
int data=((int)readBuf[1] & 0x03)<< 8|(int)readBuf[2];
```

The first part of the expression extracts the low three bits from the first byte the slave sent and as these are the most significant bits they are shifted up eight places. The rest of the bits are then ORed with them to give the full 10-bit result.

To convert to volts we use:

```
float volts=(float)data*3.3f/1023.0f;
```

assuming that VREF is 3.3V.

In a real application you would also need to convert the voltage to some other quantity such as temperature or light level.

Some Packaged Functions

This all works but it would be good to have a function that read the AtoD on a specified channel:

```
int readADC( mraa_spi_context spi,uint8_t chan){
 uint8_t buf[] = {0x01,(0x08|chan)<<4,0x00};
 uint8_t readBuf[3];
 mraa_spi_transfer_buf (spi, buf, readBuf,3);
 return ((int)readBuf[1] & 0x03) << 8 | (int) readBuf[2];
}
```

Notice that this only works if the SPI bus has been initialized and set up correctly. An initialization function is something like:

```
mraa_spi_context initADC(int freq){
mraa_spi_context spi = mraa_spi_init(0);
mraa_spi_mode(spi,  MRAA_SPI_MODE0 );
mraa_spi_frequency(spi,freq);
mraa_spi_lsbmode(spi, 0);
mraa_spi_bit_per_word(spi,8);
 return spi;
}
```

and these could be used something like:

```
mraa_spi_context spi=initADC(1000000);
int data;
data =readADC(spi,0);
printf("Data %d \n",data);
float volts=((float)data)*3.3f/1023.0f;
printf("volts= %f \n",volts);
mraa_spi_stop(spi);
```

How Fast

Once you have the basic facilities working the next question is always how fast does something work. In this case we need to know what sort or data rates we can achieve using this AtoD converter. The simplest way of finding this out is to use the fastest read loop:

```
for(;;){
 int data=readADC(0x5);
}
```

With a set clock frequency of 60KHz we get a measured clock rate of 60.1kHz the sampling rate is measured to be 1.6K sample/s which is less than the theoretical upper limit of 2.5K samples/s for 24 bits ignoring any dead time between readings. If you up the clock rate to 100KHz you will find that while the clock rate does go up to 100KHz the sample rate is only 2.3K samples/s compared to the theoretical upper limit of 4.16K samples/s.

It doesn't matter how fast you attempt to push the clock rate, even to 1MHz you can't do better than about 5K samples/s which is a fundamental bottle neck set by the software.

You can see the big gaps between reads on the logic analyzer screen dump:

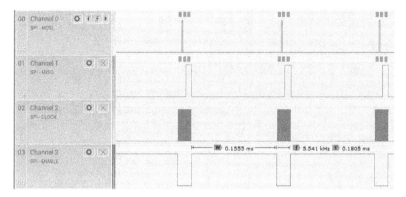

Notice that it isn't possible to increase the speed by putting multiple reads into a single transfer because the MCP3008 simply sends zeros after the third byte if the master keeps the clock running. That is you can't use something like:

```
uint8_t buf[] = {0x01,0x80,0x00,0x01,0x80,0x00};
uint8_t readBuf[6];
mraa_spi_transfer_buf (spi, buf, readBuf,6);
```

The MCP3008 returns zeros at the attempt to get it to read another sample.

Using Software SPI Emulation

One way of getting a higher sampling rate is to use the software emulation introduced at the end of the previous chapter. We could write a general n-byte transfer function, but as this is specifically aimed at reading the MCP3008 it makes more sense to write a function that transfers three bytes and reads the ADC returning the assembled value.

First we need to add the global variables specifying the GPIO lines to use:

```
mraa_gpio_context CS1;
mraa_gpio_context SCK;
mraa_gpio_context MOSI;
mraa_gpio_context MISO;
```

Next we need an initialization function and this is just the initialization code in the last chapter packaged into a function:

```
void initSPIsoft() {
CS1 = mraa_gpio_init(9);
mraa_gpio_dir(CS1, MRAA_GPIO_OUT);
mraa_gpio_use_mmaped(CS1, 1);
mraa_gpio_write(CS1, 1);
SCK = mraa_gpio_init(10);
mraa_gpio_dir(SCK, MRAA_GPIO_OUT);
mraa_gpio_use_mmaped(SCK, 1);
mraa_gpio_write(SCK, 0);
```

```
MOSI = mraa_gpio_init(11);
mraa_gpio_dir(MOSI, MRAA_GPIO_OUT);
mraa_gpio_use_mmaped(MOSI, 1);
mraa_gpio_write(MOSI, 0);MISO = mraa_gpio_init(24);
mraa_gpio_use_mmaped(MISO, 1);
mraa_gpio_dir(MISO, MRAA_GPIO_IN);
```

The read function is essentially the byte transfer function given at the end of the previous chapter but reading three bytes and only changing the CS1 line once a the start and end. The function starts off with some initialization and then it activates the CS1 line:

```
int readADCsoft(uint8_t chan, int delay) {
 int i, j;
 int read;
 int result;
 uint8_t byte;
 read = 0;
 mraa_gpio_write(CS1, 0);
 for (j = 1; j < 100; j++) {
 };
```

The first byte transfer is:

```
byte = 0x01;
for (i = 0; i < 8; i++) {
 mraa_gpio_write(MOSI, byte & 0x80);
 byte = byte << 1;
 for (j = 1; j < delay; j++) {
 };
 mraa_gpio_write(SCK, 1);
 for (j = 1; j < delay / 2; j++) {
 };
 read = read << 1;
 read = read | (mraa_gpio_read(MISO));
 for (j = 1; j < delay / 2; j++) {
 };
 mraa_gpio_write(SCK, 0);
}
```

Notice we are not interested in what the ADC sends back to us so we can simply ignore the value in read.

The second byte starts the data transfer and selects the ADC channel:

```
byte = (0x08 | chan) << 4;
for (i = 0; i < 8; i++) {
 mraa_gpio_write(MOSI, byte & 0x80);
 byte = byte << 1;
 for (j = 1; j < delay; j++) {
 };
 mraa_gpio_write(SCK, 1);
 for (j = 1; j < delay / 2; j++) {
 };
 read = read << 1;
```

```
read = read | (mraa_gpio_read(MISO));
for (j = 1; j < delay / 2; j++) {
};
mraa_gpio_write(SCK, 0);
}
result = (int) read & 0x03 << 8;
```

Notice that this time we collect the bottom two bits of the byte that the ADC sent and store them in result as the most significant bits.

The final byte is the lower eight bits of the result:

```
byte = 0;
for (i = 0; i < 8; i++) {
mraa_gpio_write(MOSI, byte & 0x80);
byte = byte << 1;
for (j = 1; j < delay; j++) {
};
mraa_gpio_write(SCK, 1);
for (j = 1; j < delay / 2; j++) {
};
read = read << 1;
read = read | (mraa_gpio_read(MISO));
for (j = 1; j < delay / 2; j++) {
};
mraa_gpio_write(SCK, 0);
}
```

Now all we have to do is deactivate the CS1 line and return the result:

```
mraa_gpio_write(CS0, 1);
for (j = 1; j < 10; j++) {
};
return result | read;
}
```

If you try this out with:

```
int data;
initSPIsoft();
for (;;) {
data = readADCsoft(0, 0);
}
```

You will discover that the clock rate is roughly 666KHz and the sample rate is roughly 24K samples per second. You can use lower sampling rates by setting a delay greater than zero.

As before, notice that this tight sampling loop means that all other processes are locked out of running on the core that your program is running on. If you need to go faster than this, the only alternative at the moment is to use some external SPI hardware.

Listing Of Soft SPI Program

The complete soft SPI program including the mraa ADC reading function is:

```c
#include <stdio.h>
#include <stdlib.h>
#include "mraa.h"
#include <unistd.h>

int readADC(mraa_spi_context spi, uint8_t chan);
mraa_spi_context initADC(int freq);
int readADCsoft(uint8_t chan, int delay);
void initSPIsoft();

mraa_gpio_context CS1;
mraa_gpio_context SCK;
mraa_gpio_context MOSI;
mraa_gpio_context MISO;

int main() {
 const struct sched_param priority = { 1 };
 sched_setscheduler(0, SCHED_FIFO, &priority);
 // mraa_spi_context spi=initADC(1000000);
 int data;
 initSPIsoft();
 for (;;) {
  // data =readADC(spi,0);
  data = readADCsoft(0, 0);
 }
 printf("Data %d \n", data);
 float volts = ((float) data) * 3.3f / 1023.0f;
 printf("volts= %f \n", volts);
 // mraa_spi_stop(spi);
 return 0;
}

int readADC(mraa_spi_context spi, uint8_t chan) {
 uint8_t buf[] = {0x01,(0x08 | chan) << 4, 0x00};
 uint8_t readBuf[3];
 mraa_spi_transfer_buf(spi, buf, readBuf, 3);
 return ((int) readBuf[1] & 0x03) << 8 | (int) readBuf[2];
}

mraa_spi_context initADC(int freq) {
 mraa_spi_context spi =
 mraa_spi_init(0);mraa_spi_mode(spi, MRAA_SPI_MODE0);
 mraa_spi_frequency(spi, freq);
 mraa_spi_lsbmode(spi, 0);
 mraa_spi_bit_per_word(spi, 8);
 return spi;
}
int readADCsoft(uint8_t chan, int delay) {
 int i, j;
```

```
int read;
int result;
uint8_t byte;
read = 0;
mraa_gpio_write(CS1, 0);
for (j = 1; j < 100; j++) {
};
byte = 0x01;
for (i = 0; i < 8; i++) {
 mraa_gpio_write(MOSI, byte & 0x80);
 byte = byte << 1;
 for (j = 1; j < delay; j++) {
 };
 mraa_gpio_write(SCK, 1);
 for (j = 1; j < delay / 2; j++) {
 };
 read = read << 1;
 read = read | (mraa_gpio_read(MISO));
 for (j = 1; j < delay / 2; j++) {
 };
 mraa_gpio_write(SCK, 0);
}
byte = (0x08 | chan) << 4;
for (i = 0; i < 8; i++) {
 mraa_gpio_write(MOSI, byte & 0x80);
 byte = byte << 1;
 for (j = 1; j < delay; j++) {
 };
 mraa_gpio_write(SCK, 1);
 for (j = 1; j < delay / 2; j++) {
 };
 read = read << 1;
 read = read | (mraa_gpio_read(MISO));
 for (j = 1; j < delay / 2; j++) {
 };
 mraa_gpio_write(SCK, 0);
}
result = (int) read & 0x03 << 8;
byte = 0;
for (i = 0; i < 8; i++) {
 mraa_gpio_write(MOSI, byte & 0x80);
 byte = byte << 1;
 for (j = 1; j < delay; j++) {
 };
 mraa_gpio_write(SCK, 1);
 for (j = 1; j < delay / 2; j++) {
 };
 read = read << 1;
 read = read | (mraa_gpio_read(MISO));
 for (j = 1; j < delay / 2; j++) {
 };
 mraa_gpio_write(SCK, 0);
}
mraa_gpio_write(CS0, 1);
```

```
  for (j = 1; j < 10; j++) {
  };
  return result | read;
}

void initSPIsoft() {
 CS1 = mraa_gpio_init(9);
 mraa_gpio_dir(CS1, MRAA_GPIO_OUT);
 mraa_gpio_use_mmaped(CS1, 1);
 mraa_gpio_write(CS1, 1);

 SCK = mraa_gpio_init(10);
 mraa_gpio_dir(SCK, MRAA_GPIO_OUT);
 mraa_gpio_use_mmaped(SCK, 1);
 mraa_gpio_write(SCK, 0);

 MOSI = mraa_gpio_init(11);
 mraa_gpio_dir(MOSI, MRAA_GPIO_OUT);
 mraa_gpio_use_mmaped(MOSI, 1);
 mraa_gpio_write(MOSI, 0);

 MISO = mraa_gpio_init(24);
 mraa_gpio_use_mmaped(MISO, 1);
 mraa_gpio_dir(MISO, MRAA_GPIO_IN);
 }
```

Summary

1. Making SPI work with any particular device has four steps:
    i. Discover how to connect the device to the SPI.
       This is a matter of identifying pinouts and mostly what chip selects are supported.
    ii. Find out how to configure the SPI bus to work with the device. This is mostly a matter of clock speed and mode.
    iii. Identify the commands that you need to send to the device to get it to do something and what data it sends back as a response.
    iv. Find, or workout, what the relationship between the raw reading, the voltage and the quantity the voltage represents is.
2. The Edison has some problems running the SPI bus at high data rates if you cannot group the transaction into a larger block transfer. For the MCP3008 this isn't possible.
3. Using mraa the fastest data sampling rate from the MCP3008 is 5K samples per second.
4. Using a software simulated SPI bus you can achieve rates of just less than 25K samples per second.

Chapter 15

Beyond Mraa- Controlling Features It Doesn't

There is a Linux-based approach to working with GPIO lines and serial buses that is worth knowing about because it provides an alternative to using the mraa library. Sometimes you need this because you are working in a language for which mraa isn't available. It also lets you access features that mraa doesn't make available.

A key principle of Linux is that everything is a file or a folder. As much as is possible, Linux deals with external hardware by treating it as if it was a file system. This is reasonable because external hardware either wants to receive data as commands or something to store or display, or it want to send data as responses or user input. So most hardware interacts with Linux as a source or a sink of data, and this is exactly what a file is all about.

This "everything is a file" approach only really fails when issues of performance enter the picture. Accessing a piece of hardware as if it was a file when it isn't can be slow. In normal use mraa accesses most of the hardware of the Edison using file commands, but when you use fast memory access it maps the hardware into user space and accesses it as a range of memory locations.

So file-based access to the hardware can be slow, but it has the huge advantage that it is language-independent. Every language has the facilities needed to open, read/write and close a file and so has the facilities needed to work with hardware via the file system

The big problem is that the details of how hardware is represented as a file system is poorly documented and you have to find out about it by guessing, trial and error, reverse engineering, or by reading code the makes use of it.

Working with SYSFS

SYSFS is a virtual file system that provides all sorts of access to hardware and the operation of the Linux kernel. You can spend a lot of time exploring it, but the only part we are particularly interested in is the gpio folder. SYSFS is usually mounted in the sys folder and the folder that corresponds to the gpio device is usually:

```
/sys/class/gpio
```

To see what is in the folder, simply list it:

```
ls /sys/class/gpio
```

```
root@edison:/# ls /sys/class/gpio
export    gpio114  gpio125  gpio128  gpio131  gpio134
gpio109  gpio115  gpio126  gpio129  gpio132  gpiochip0
gpio111  gpio124  gpio127  gpio130  gpio133  unexport
```

These are the gpio lines that are already in use by some process or other. Notice that the gpio numbers are not mraa numbers, but SYSFS numbers.

The steps in using a line are always the same:

- Reserve or "export" the gpio line so that no other process can use it
- Set its direction and read or write it
- Unreserve it or unexport it

You can do these steps from any language that supports file operations including the shell.

To reserve a gpio line you have to write its number to the export folder and you can do this using the shell command. For example, assuming we want to work with gpio-44:

```
echo 44 > /sys/class/gpio/export
```

You can of course change 44 to any valid gpio number.

You can do the same job in C:

```
gpio=44;
fd = open("/sys/class/gpio/export", O_WRONLY);
sprintf(buf, "%d", gpio);
write(fd, buf, strlen(buf));
close(fd);
```

If you are not familiar with C file operations - the **open** function opens export for write only, the **sprintf** command creates a string with the number of the gpio line and then this is written to the file before it is closed.

Once you have the pin reserved you will see a new folder, **gpio44**, corresponding to it in **/sys/class/gpio**.

Now that you have it reserved, you can set its direction and read or write it. To do this read or write to the appropriate sub folder of the new gpio folder, direction or value.

For example, to read the line use:

```
echo "in" > /sys/class/gpio/gpio44/direction
cat /sys/class/gpio/gpio44/value
```

and to set the line high and then low:

```
echo "out" > /sys/class/gpio/gpio44/direction
echo 1 > /sys/class/gpio/gpio44/value
echo 0 > /sys/class/gpio/gpio4/value
```

You can do the same things using C but it is slightly more verbose due to the need to open and close files and build the appropriate strings.

Example - toggling a line

As an example consider the following C program which sets gpio-44 to output and then toggles it high and low as fast as possible:

```c
#include <stdio.h>
#include <stdlib.h>
#include "mraa.h"
int main() {
 int fd;
 char buf[100];
 int gpio = 44;
 fd = open("/sys/class/gpio/export", O_WRONLY);
 sprintf(buf, "%d", gpio);
 write(fd, buf, strlen(buf));
 close(fd);
 sprintf(buf, "/sys/class/gpio/gpio%d/direction", gpio);
 fd = open(buf, O_WRONLY);
 write(fd, "out", 3);
 close(fd);
 sprintf(buf, "/sys/class/gpio/gpio%d/value", gpio);
 fd = open(buf, O_WRONLY);
 for(;;){
  write(fd, "1", 1);
  write(fd, "0", 1);
 }
 close(fd);
 fd = open("/sys/class/gpio/unexport", O_WRONLY);
 sprintf(buf, "%d", gpio);
 write(fd, buf, strlen(buf));
 close(fd);

 return 0;
}
```

Notice the "clever" use of **sprintf** to create strings which incorporate the number of the GPIO line you are using.

189

It you try this this out you will discover that the pulse train has a frequency of 50KHz and a pulse width of 10 microseconds. Which is comparable to mraa in non-memory-mapped mode.

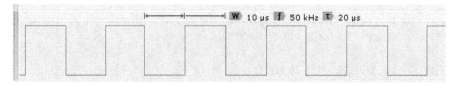

So there is little to be gained from using SYSFS in this way - it is more a matter of knowing it is there. It is worth knowing that if you plan to read a GPIO line using this technique after the first read you need to position the file pointer back to the start of the file to read subsequent values:

```
lseek(fp, 0, SEEK_SET);
```

Controlling the GPIO Mode

In principle you should be able to set the output mode of the GPIO lines using mraa but at the moment you can't and mraa wound not support the full range of possibilities even if it did work. There should be additional folders in the **sys/class/gpio** directories that allow you to control the configuration of the gpio line - pullup, pulldown etc. but these aren't present.

Instead there are directories in **sys/kernel/debug/** that do the same job. Why they are in the debugfs is not clear as they are generally useful and not particularly to do with debugging. The debugfs is usually not enabled in Linux and you have to recompile the kernel to enable it, but it is enabled in the standard distribution of the Edison firmware.

If you get a list of all the folders in **sys/kernel/debug/gpio_debug** you will see that there is a folder for each gpio line. If you list all the folders in one of these, for example:

```
ls /sys/kernel/debug/gpio_debug/gpio44
```

you will see a the following list of folders that relate to the configuration of the pin:

```
current_debounce
available_debounce
current_direction
available_direction
current_irqtype
available_irqtype
current_opendrain
available_opendrain
current_override_indir
available_override_indir
current_override_inval
available_override_inval
```

```
current_override_outdir
available_override_outdir
current_override_outval
available_override_outval
current_pinmux
available_pinmux
current_pullmode
available_pullmode
current_pullstrength
available_pullstrength
current_standby_indir
available_standby_indir
current_standby_inval
available_standby_inval
current_standby_opendrain
available_standby_opendrain
current_standby_outdir
available_standby_outdir
current_standby_outval
available_standby_outval
current_standby_pullmode
available_standby_pullmode
current_standby_trigger
available_standby_trigger
current_value
available_value irq_count
conf_reg register_info
```

You can see that they are mostly in **current** and **available** pairs. The contents in **current** give you the value already in set and those in **available** give you the possible values you can set.

Three of the files relate to the mode of operation of the pin:

```
available_pullmode nopull pullup pulldown
available_pullstrength 2k 20k 50k 910ohms
available_opendrain disable enable
```

The current values of these are **pullup 50k** and **disable**.

You might at this point think that this means that the default gpio pin configuration is 50K pullup but it isn't. The fact that open_drain is disabled sets the pin into push-pull output mode and the pullup and 50k are ignored.

If you want to experiment setting the output modes then you can use **cat** and **echo** at the command line, but you need to know that if you make use of the SYSFS system to change the state of the gpio line then the mode is set back to push-pull automatically. This is presumably why mraa's mode setting function seems not to work.

It isn't difficult to write some functions that let you set the output mode of a pin.

The Output Modes

Before we get to the code to do the job it is worth spending a moment explaining the three basic output modes.

In push-pull mode two transistors of opposite polarity are used, for example:

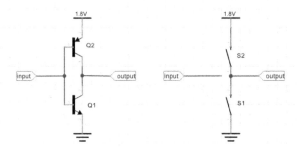

The circuit behaves like the two-switch equivalent shown on the right. Only one of the transistors, or switches, is "closed" at any time. If the input is high then Q1 is saturated and the output is connected to ground - exactly as if S1 was closed. If the input is low then Q2 is saturated and it is as if S2 was closed and the output is connected to 1.8V.

You can see that this pushes the output line high with the same "force" as it pulls it low. The Edison can source or sink up to 2mA.

The pullup mode replaces one of the transistors by a resistor:

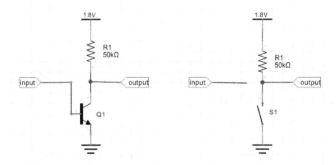

In this case the circuit is equivalent to having a single switch. When the switch is closed the output line is connected to ground and hence driven low. When the switch is open the output line is pulled high by the resistor.

You can see that in this case the degree of pull-down is greater than the pullup, where the current is limited by the resistor. The advantage of this mode is that it can be used in an AND configuration. If multiple GPIO or other lines are connected to the output, then any one of them being low will pull the output line low. Only when all of them are off does the resistor succeed in pulling the line high. This is used, for example, in a serial bus configuration like the I2C bus.

Finally the pulldown mode is exactly the same as the pullup only now the resistor is used to pull the output line low:

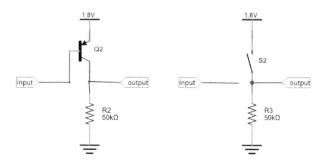

In the case of the pulldown mode the line is held high by the transistor but pulled low by the resistor only when all the switches are open. Putting this the other way round - the line is high if any one switch is closed.

Generally speaking the push-pull mode is best for driving general loads, motors, LEDs, etc. The pullup/down modes are used where you need to create a serial bus of some sort or when the load needs this sort of drive.

Setting the Mode

We can use the **sys/kernel/debug/gpio_debug** file system to set the mode. First we need some general functions that read and write to the file system starting with a function that will read the current property of any pin:

```
void getSetting(int pin,char prop[],char* buf){
 sprintf(buf,"/sys/kernel/debug/gpio_debug/gpio%d/current_%s",
                                                  pin,prop);
 int fd = open(buf, O_RDONLY);
 int count=read(fd, buf, 10);
 buf[count]=0;
 close(fd);
}
```

Notice that the property is specified by **prop[]** and the result returned in **buf[]**.

Similarly we need a function that will write a new value to any current property for the specified pin:

```
void putSetting(int pin,char prop[],char value[]){
 char buf[200];
 sprintf(buf,
     "/sys/kernel/debug/gpio_debug/gpio%d/current_%s",
     pin,prop);
 int fd = open(buf, O_WRONLY);
 write(fd, value, strlen(value));
 close(fd);
}
```

Using the **getSetting** function it is now easy to write a function that will print the current mode status to the console;

```
void getMode(int pin){
 char buf[200];
 getSetting(pin,"pullmode",buf);
 printf("pullmode= %s \n",buf);
 getSetting(pin,"pullstrength",buf);
 printf("pullstrength= %s \n",buf);
 getSetting(pin,"opendrain",buf);
 printf("opendrain= %s \n",buf);
}
```

This is useful when you are debugging to see what mode is set and to make sure that mraa isn't changing it while you are not looking.

The problem is that if you use mraa to set a pin to high or low then the use of SYSFS will reset the mode. The solution to this problem is to use memory mapped access which mraa supports and doesn't use SYSFS.

For example:

```
int gpio = 44;
mraa_gpio_context pin = mraa_gpio_init(31);
mraa_gpio_dir(pin, MRAA_GPIO_OUT);
mraa_gpio_use_mmaped(pin, 1);
putSetting(gpio,"pullmode","pullup");
putSetting(gpio,"pullstrength","50k");
putSetting(gpio,"opendrain","enable");
getMode(gpio);
mraa_gpio_write(pin, 1);
mraa_gpio_write(pin, 0);
getMode(gpio);
```

Recall that GPIO-44 is the same as mraa pin 31 so we are working with the same pin in all of the code. First we set the pin to output and memory mapped access using mraa functions. Next we set the output mode to **50K pullup** and enable the opendrain mode. You can see from the output that the pin is written to and the set mode doesn't change.

If you change **use_mmaped** to

```
        mraa_gpio_use_mmaped(pin, 1);
```

then you will find that the mode changes between setting the pin high and low.

You can check that the mode really has changed by connecting a multimeter to the pin and measuring its voltage.

In push-pull mode, i.e. with

```
putSetting(gpio,"opendrain","disable");
```

the output voltage will be a little over 1.8V, but with it enabled it drops to just over 1.7V. You can also put a 10K resistor from the pin to ground and you will discover that the voltage drops to around 2.7, which is correct for a voltage divider consisting of a 50K pullup and a 10K load resistor.

All of the pullstrength resistors, work but something strange happens if you specify 910ohms - the output voltage drops.

You can also try making pulldown work - it doesn't seem to. However, setting pullmode to **nopull** gives you the open drain output line without a pullup resistor. This allows you to add an external pull up resistor of your own choice between the output line and th 1.8V line.

To summarize:

You can work with two modes:

- If current_opendrain is set to disable then you have a pushpull output stage - this is the default for all output pins.
- If current_opendrain is set to enable then you can set pullmode to pullup with built in resistors of 50K, 20K and 2K or you can set pullup pullmode to nopull and use your own external pull up resistors.

There may well be other things that are useful in SYSFS and in **/sys/kernel/debug/gpio_debug/gpio**,

but there is currently no documentation for it.

Summary

1. Most if not all Linux devices are presented as if they were a file system. The same is true of the Edison's GPIO lines and you can find these in SYSFS.

2. Using standard file handling commands you can control the GPIO lines from almost any programming language.

3. The disadvantage of SYSFS is that it is slow.

4. The kernel/debug file system has additional folders that allow you to control the GPIO output mode.

5. You need to make use of the output mode settings whenever you need to select and open collector output.

Alphabetical Index

1.8V logic..12, 15-16, 105, 115-117, 123-124
10-bit AtoD...171
1uF capacitor..172
2N2222...88, 117-118, 130
anti-aliasing filter...173
Arduino..9
Arduino breakout board..12-14, 39-40, 82, 97, 115
Arduino sketch..40
bcm2835 library...175
Bipolar Junction Transistor, BJT...........................88, 117-119, 122, 137
bit-banging...55
blink an LED..29
Bluetooth...9
breakpoint..36-37
busy wait...57-59, 61-64, 142-144, 166
C...27
C++..27
checksum...112-114
checksum function...113
Chip Enable/Select lines...154
clock rate...101
clock stretching protocol...101
clock_gettime...51-52, 64
Configure_Edison utility...22-23
CRC...113-114, 149
debounce...51-52, 190
Delay Using usleep..57
DHT11,..127
DHT22...127
DMA..80, 164, 170, 175
DS18B20...137
DtoA converter..94
Eclipse IDE...28-30, 32, 36-38, 46-48
Edison breakout board,..14
emitter follower configuration..92
FDN327B...116
FET (Field Effect Transistor),..88, 116, 122
FIFO (First In First Out)...............73-75, 77-80, 134-135, 141, 150, 168, 182
Flash Tool Lite...21
Galileo..12

GPIO..39, 81
    fast input...63
    FIFO scheduling group..165
    input...46
    Linux task scheduling...51
    memory mapped I/O....................55, 60, 63, 69, 81, 82, 129, 137
    output mode..43
    pin configuration...191
    scheduling...71-75, 77, 78
    Viper RTOS...72
    write 44
Hirose DF40...12
HTU21D..105
humidity...105-114, 127, 133-135
I/O connector..10, 12
I2C bus.......................40, 41, 93, 95-103, 105-114, 121, 193
    HTU21D...105
    No hold master mode...110
    SCL..40, 41, 96, 97, 101, 106
    SCL,..95
    SDA..40, 95-97, 106, 128
IC voltage translator...173
Integrated installer..19, 21, 28-29
Intel IoT Developer Kit..29
Intel System Studio IoT Edition...28, 38
interrupt...39, 47-51, 53, 54, 63, 71
Maxim 1-Wire bus...137
MCP3000 family of AtoD converters......................................171
MCP3008...171, 173, 179, 185
MCU..10, 11, 27, 55, 71, 72
memory mapped I/O......................55, 60-63, 69, 81-82, 129, 137
Micro B to A USB cable..17
mini-breakout board.......................14-17, 24, 25, 82, 105, 115
MISO (Master Input Slave Output)...............41, 154, 160-169, 179-184
MOSFET...116-119
MOSI Master Output Slave Input................41, 154 160-169, 179-184
mraa library...24, 32, 156
multimeter..25
npn transistor...117
open collector bus...96, 121-122, 138
open collector mode..122
open collector/no pullup resistor...141
opendrain mode..194

opkg...23
overrun errors..163
Phased Pulses...44
polling...46, 47, 49, 53, 54, 63, 64, 66, 101
precision voltage reference chip...172
pulldown mode...193
pullup mode..192
pullup resistors..96
Pulse Width Measurement..50
push-pull mode...192
Pulse Width Modulation PWM...40, 80-94
    duty cycle..87
    How Fast..86
    LED..88
    servo..91-93, 118-120
    uses..87, 94
Python..16, 24-27
realtime scheduling...75
Remote Systems..31, 35
Round Robin...74
SCHED_FIFO..73
SCHED_OTHER...73
SCHED_RR...74
Schottky diode...175
SCL clock rate...101
SCLK...154, 155, 174
scratchpad memory..148
serial bus...95
serial port...10, 19-22
servo circuit..118
single-transistor level shifter.............................122, 129, 139
Slave Select lines..154
SMI...79
software emulation of SPI bus...164
speed up capacitor...175
SPI bus.........................153-158, 160-165, 169-171, 173-176, 185
SSH..20, 22, 31, 32, 35
successive approximation converter...172
SYSFS................39-45, 49-50, 59-61, 63-69, 82-83, 154, 187-195
temperature.........................105-114, 127, 133-137, 147-148, 151
UART...80
USB cable..17
USB port..12, 17-18

usleep................45-46, 51-52, 57-58, 61, 77, 89-91, 131, 135, 142, 147, 152
Viper RTOS...72
WiFi...9-10, 12-13, 22, 30-32, 79
wire or bus..121
Yocto Linux...10, 19-23, 31, 56, 72, 163
Zener diode..172

www.ingramcontent.com/pod-product-compliance
Lightning Source LLC
LaVergne TN
LVHW062316060326
832902LV00013B/2254